Study Guide to Accompany

RESEARCH METHODS IN PSYCHOLOGY
Fourth Edition

David G. Elmes
Washington and Lee University

Barry H. Kantowitz
Battelle Memorial Institute

Henry L. Roediger III
Rice University

Prepared by
Joseph B. Thompson
Washington and Lee University

David G. Payne
State University of New York-Binghampton

WEST PUBLISHING COMPANY
St. Paul   New York   Los Angeles   San Francisco

ISBN 0–314–00205–7

Contents

Acknowledgement

Heather Turner: Thanks for your energy, hard work, good humor, and grammatical skills. We both know that you did the hard stuff.   And if you think that I'm going to claim responsibility for any remaining errors, you're wrong.

M. S.:   Thanks for your long-distance patience and encouragement from behind your editor's desk. And thanks for reordering my priorities. I'll try to remember that books are more important than contracts, and that both are less important than Thanksgiving vacations.

CHAPTER 1.
Beginning Psychological Research

SUMMARY

People do psychological research both to understand why people and animals act the way they do, and also to solve practical problems. An understanding and appreciation of the research process is necessary to conduct sound research and to evaluate the research of others.

Psychologists use the experimental method in order to be able to attribute changes in behavior (the dependent variable) to manipulations of the environment (the independent variable). If the experiment is properly performed, the effects of other variables which might influence the dependent variable are minimized though experimental design or by holding them constant.

You can get an idea for a research project from observing your own behavior or that of people around you, reading and listening. If you are curious about "why?" or "how come?" or "what would happen if...?", then you have begun the research process.

Before designing your study, it is a good idea to do some further reading to see what other researchers have found out about the problem of interest. A good way to begin the literature review is to consult the *Psychological Abstracts*. Once you are familiar with the relevant terminology, a computerized literature search is extremely helpful.

Your research question should be posed as a testable hypothesis, that is, a statement about how you think your dependent and independent variables are related, and how these variables are to be measured in your study.

Finally, before conducting the actual study, you will probably find it useful to engage in pilot research to decide on effective levels of your independent variable and to identify and correct any problems in your experimental procedure.

KEY TERMS

behavior

computerized literature search

confounding

control variable

critic

critical thinker

dependent variable

independent variable

pilot research

Psychological Abstracts

Social Science Citation Index

Stroop effect

testable hypothesis

PROGRAMMED REVIEW

1. _____ refers to overt activities of people and animals.

2. Psychologists conduct research for two basic reasons: to develop theoretical _____ of a behavior of interest, and to solve _____ _____.

3. A _____ is a person who makes an informed or reasoned judgment about the value of something.

4. In an experiment, the _____ _____ is deliberately manipulated to determine its effect on behavior.

5.   The _____ _____ is the aspect of behavior that
     is measured in a psychological experiment.

6.   _____ _____ are held constant so that they will
     not inadvertently influence the behavior of interest in an
     experiment.

7.   _____ occurs when a variable not of interest happens
     to change together with changes in the independent
     variable.

8.   Science begins with _____ - both as a source of data
     and as a source for research ideas.

9.   Professors and other _____ may suggest research
     projects, or help you refine your own research ideas.

10. The _____ _____ is a good general resource
     that will help you find journal articles relevant to your
     research ideas.

11. After you have identified a problem or idea to
     investigate, the next step is to formulate a _____
     _____.

12. Hypotheses will not be testable unless they include
     variables that are both _____ and _____.

13. In addition to suggesting ideas, a _____ _____
     will help you discover what is already known about your
     hypothesis.

14. Another name for preliminary research is _____
     research.

EXPERIMENTAL PROJECT

     One of the best ways to learn what it takes to conduct a
research project is to actually design and carry out your own
research. However, you can get a good idea of the problems
associated with conducting research by going through the
research process up to the point of actually collecting data.
Presented below are two possible research ideas. Select one of
these ideas and then attempt to design a research project to

address one (or more) of the issues raised by this problem. Be sure to formulate a testable hypothesis, perform at least a brief review of the relevant literature and determine if pilot research is necessary. Finally, design a project that would be feasible to conduct given the resources available to you.

Problem 1. A number of memory improvement books (e.g. Higbee, 1977) state that mental imagery helps people to remember. What type of evidence could we obtain that might help us determine how valid this claim is?

Problem 2. One of your friends claims that football players are better athletes than gymnasts or swimmers. Is there any evidence to support this claim? What type of research would be needed to address this issue?

REFERENCE

Higbee, K. L.(1977). *Your Memory: How it Works and How to Improve it*. Englewood Cliffs, N.J.: Prentice Hall.

EXPERIMENTAL DILEMMA

A counseling psychologist believes that physical exercise will help patients suffering from chronic depression. The psychologist is currently treating 39 people who are suffering from chronic depression. Thirty-six of these people said that they would be willing to participate in an experiment if the experiment might help them and might also provide information that would help the psychologist to learn more about how to help depressed people.

The psychologist administered a standard paper and pencil test to measure how depressed his subjects were before treatment. The psychologist used these scores to match 12 groups of three people who scored about the same on the depression test. These three people were then randomly assigned to treatment conditions.

People in condition 1 were then asked to engage in some sort of outdoors exercise three times a week, people in condition 2 exercised five times a week, and people in condition 3 were not asked to exercise, but they were asked to spend some time outdoors at least three times a week.

At the end of the six week experiment the subjects took another paper and pencil depression test. The results showed that all subjects were now rated as less depressed than they were at the beginning of the experiment. However, the subjects in conditions 1 and 2 had improved more than the subjects in condition 3. Subjects in conditions 1 and 2 had improved the same amount over the six week period.

The psychologist concluded that exercise provides help above and beyond that provided by simply spending time outdoors. He also concluded that three days of exercise a week was enough to benefit the depressed person.

What was the hypothesis tested by the researcher? What were the independent and dependent variables? What did the experimenter attempt to control in this study? How was this control achieved?

Do you agree with the conclusions drawn by this researcher? If you had to design a study to test the hypothesis under consideration, how would you design your study? Is your design better than that described above?

MULTIPLE CHOICE QUESTIONS

_____ 1. When psychologists use the word <u>behavior</u> they mean
   a. act right! As in "Behave yourself!"
   b. observable overt activities of people and animals.
   c. covert psychological processes.
   d. both b and c

_____ 2. Covert psychological processes
   a. can never be studied by psychologists.
   b. can be observed and measured directly.
   c. can be studied indirectly by measuring overt behavior.
   d. are imaginary.

_____ 3. In the demonstration experiment on reading and counting, the fastest condition was
   a. reading digits
   b. counting +'s
   c. counting digits
   d. there were no differences among these conditions

_____ 4. In the demonstration experiment on reading and counting, the slowest condition was
   a. reading digits.
   b. counting +'s.
   c. counting digits.
   d. there were no differences among these conditions

_____ 5. Experimental psychologists engage in research
   a. to help develop theoretical understanding of the phenomenon of interest.
   b. to solve practical problems.
   c. because their professor requires it.
   d. two of the above.

_____ 6. A critic
   a. makes informed or reasoned judgements.
   b. finds fault with the work of others.
   c. is less objective than an evaluator.
   d. is one who is unable to engage in research directly.

_____ 7. In an experiment, the independent variable is
    a. manipulated by the experimenter.
    b. measured by the experimenter.
    c. held constant.
    d. two of the above

_____ 8. In an experiment, the dependent variable is
    a. manipulated by the experimenter.
    b. measured by the experimenter.
    c. held constant.
    d. two of the above

_____ 9. In an experiment, a control variable is
    a. manipulated by the experimenter.
    b. measured by the experimenter.
    c. held constant.
    d. two of the above

_____10. When some aspect of an experiment changes along with changes in the independent variable,
    a. you are more likely to get interpretable results.
    b. you are more likely to get large behavioral effects.
    c. confederation has occurred.
    d. confounding has occurred.

_____11. In the demonstration experiment of the Stroop effect, what was confounded with the levels of the independent variable?
    a. response time
    b. task differences
    c. task ordering
    d. response ordering

_____12. Research ideas can come from
    a. consulting with an expert.
    b. reading journal articles.
    c. identifying practical problems.
    d. all of the above

_____13. In which of the following sources would you <u>not</u> generally expect to find review articles?

a. *American Psychologist*

b. *Journal of Experimental Psychology: General*

c. *Journal of Experimental Social Psychology*

d. *Psychological Bulletin*

e. *Psychological Review*

_____14. Which of the following does <u>not</u> present article abstracts?

a. *Biological Abstracts*

b. *Ergonomics Abstracts*

c. *Index Medicus*

d. *Psychological Abstracts*

e. none of the above

_____15. Perhaps the best place to start in developing a list of references for a problem in psychology that is new to you is:

a. *American Journal of Psychology.*

b. *The American Psychologist.*

c. *Annual Review of Psychology.*

d. *Psychological Abstracts.*

e. *Psychological Review.*

_____16. A journal that allows you to identify recent articles that have referenced a critical key article is

a. *Current Contents.*

b. *Annual Review of Psychology.*

c. *Bulletin of the Psychonomic Society.*

d. *Social Science Citation Index.*

_____17. A statement about a presumed or theoretical relationship between two or more variables, and includes a description of how these variables are to be measured is called a

    a. psychological theory.

    b. research design.

    c. citation abstract.

    d. testable hypothesis.

_____18. In addition to providing research ideas, a literature search is useful in finding out

    a. if your research hypothesis has already been studied.

    b. useful "tricks of the trade" in designing your experiment.

    c. both a and b

    d. none of the above

_____19. Preliminary research performed beginning a full-scale experiment

    a. is called pilot research.

    b. allows you to get the bugs out of your experimental procedure.

    c. allows you to identify useful levels of your independent variable.

    d. all of the above

TRUE-FALSE QUESTIONS

_____ 1. There is no reason to learn about research, unless you personally plan to conduct research.

_____ 2. It is possible for research findings to be useful, even if they don't increase our theoretical understanding.

_____ 3. If confounding has occurred, the effect of the independent variable is always overestimated.

_____ 4. If the same people are all tested under several experimental conditions, testing different people with different orders of these conditions will reduce the condition-order confounding.

_____ 5. *Psychological Abstracts* lists the titles of articles from almost all journals that publish psychological research.

_____ 6. If the variables mentioned in an hypothesis are not measurable, the hypothesis is not testable.

ESSAY QUESTIONS

1. Ask at least three questions based on the Stroop phenomenon. Select one of these questions and discuss each of the steps you might go through in developing a research project to answer this question.

2. Are the same steps involved in developing research to increase theoretical understanding as in developing research to answer a practical question? Explain.

Chapter 2
Explanation in Scientific Psychology

SUMMARY

The chapter describes several ways in which our beliefs about the world may be fixed. Each of these methods differs in their relative level of sophistication. The simplest method is the method of authority whereby the word of some higher authority, such as a parent or media figure, is taken to be true. With the method of tenacity, people refuse to alter their beliefs regardless of evidence to the contrary. Statements might also be believed if they sound reasonable a priori. In contrast with these methods, the scientific method is based on systematic empirical observation. Thus with the scientific method, belief is based on experience, and beliefs that are inconsistent with this experience can be discarded.

A theory may be defined as a set of related statements that explains a variety of occurrences. Theories serve two primary functions. First, they help to organize existing data. Second, theories may be used to generate predictions for situations where no data have yet been obtained.

Although data and theory are integral parts of all scientific investigations, some approaches tend to emphasize one over the other. The inductive approach emphasizes the collection of data with the hope that general principles will emerge once enough data are collected. An alternative approach, the deductive approach, primarily involves research that is guided by some theoretical explanation(s) of a particular set of phenomena. While neither of these approaches is infallible, a combination of induction and deduction allows science to progress to a more thorough understanding of nature.

Theories can be evaluated and compared on several bases. A good theory should (a) be precisely stated, (b) contain as few statements as possible to account for the phenomena of interest, and (c) be testable. Theories may include intervening variables that serve to connect theoretical concepts to observables, and may provide economy of explanation. A theory may be disproved by data that are inconsistent with the predictions of the theory. However, theories can never be proven to be correct, since it is possible that data that has not yet been collected could eventually disprove the theory.

Research in science is often divided into two categories-- basic and applied. Basic research is conducted in order to establish a wide data base for future reference. Basic research is not generally conducted to solve a specified problem but rather is conducted to provide additional knowledge about a set of events or processes. Applied research, on the other hand, is directed explicitly at solving a particular problem in an applied (i.e., real world) setting. Applied researchers use knowledge gained in basic research in their work, although the time lag between the original observations in basic research and the eventual application of this knowledge to the real world may be quite long.

KEY TERMS

a priori method	method of authority
applied research	method of tenacity
basic research	organization
data	parsimony
deduction	prediction
diffusion of responsibility	scientific method
empirical	self-correcting
falsifiability view	strong inference
intervening variable	testability
induction	theory

PROGRAMMED REVIEW

1.   The phenomenon of people working less hard in groups than alone is called _____ _____.

2. Social loafing may be a special case of a more general social phenomenon called _____ of _____.

3. According to the American philosopher Charles Sanders Pierce, the simplest way of fixing belief is the method of _____.

4. The method of fixing beliefs in which one refuses to alter their acquired knowledge regardless of evidence to the contrary is known as the method of _____.

5. In the scientific method of fixing beliefs, beliefs are fixed on the basis of _____.

6. Scientific psychology is characterized as being _____ and _____ -correcting.

7. The two most important elements shared by all approaches to science are _____ and _____.

8. In the inductive approach to science, reasoning proceeds from particular _____ to a general _____. The opposite occurs in the _____ approach to science.

9. The _____ scientist believes that general explanatory principles will emerge once enough data have been collected.

10. According to the _____ approach to theories, data are useful only in the evaluation of a theoretical explanation.

11. According to Popper, the philosopher of science, good theories must be _____.

12. Experiments designed to pit two hypotheses against each other in the hope of eliminating one of them involve the process of _____ _____.

13. One function of a theory is to provide a framework for _____ existing data.

14. Theories may be used to generate _____ for situations where no data have yet been obtained.

15. The two functions of a theory known as organization and prediction are sometimes called _____ and _____, respectively.

16. An abstract concept that relates independent and dependent variables is called an _____ _____.

17. Intervening variables, by reducing the number of links necessary to relate independent and dependent variables, provide _____ in explanation.

18. A good theory will make very _____ predictions.

19. In evaluating theories, the criterion of _____ holds that the fewer the concepts a theory needs to explain various phenomena, the better the theory.

20. Theories having mathematical formulations are said to have greater _____ than those using only verbal statements.

21. A theory that cannot be _____ can never be disproved.

22. What distinguishes one science from another is the different _____ that are used.

23. Psychologists try to understand the underlying _____ that lead to behavior rather than the physical situations that produce behaviors.

EXPERIMENTAL PROJECT

Suppose that someone comes to you with an infinitely large deck of cards. Each card contains a geometric shape (circle, square, or triangle) on one side and a color patch (red, green, or yellow) on the other. The person with the cards tells you that each card with a circle on one side has either a green or a blue patch on the other side. Your task is to test this "theory" in any way you wish, with the restriction that you may only turn over one card at a time. What sort of "evidence" would you consider critical in testing this theory? How many cards would you need to see before you believed the theory? Would your answer to these questions change if the person stated that 9 out of 10 cards with a circle on one side have a green or blue patch on the other side?

EXPERIMENTAL DILEMMA

Two researchers are studying the effects of marijuana on personal motivation. Both experimenters believe that chronic marijuana use is associated with a decline in motivation level, but they have different ways of studying the problem. Research

A hypothesizes that "Grade point average decreases logarithmically with the number of marijuana cigarettes smoked per week." Researcher B's hypothesis states that "People who smoke marijuana have less drive to succeed than people who do not smoke marijuana." Which experimenter has a better research hypothesis? Why?

MULTIPLE CHOICE QUESTIONS

_____ 1. The tendency of people to work less hard in groups is known as

a. diffusion of effort.

b. social irresponsibility.

c. social loafing.

d. good sense.

_____ 2. Experiments have shown that people work just as hard in a group as when they work alone if

a. good performance is rewarded.

b. "team spirit" is high.

c. the group leader is autocratic.

d. each individual's performance is monitored.

_____ 3. The simplest way of fixing beliefs is

a. the a priori method.

b. the method of authority.

c. the method of tenacity.

d. the scientific method.

_____ 4. After listening to a lecture by an astronaut who conducted experiments aboard the space shuttle, you now believe that plants can germinate in space. This belief was fixed by

a. the method of authority.

b. the method of tenacity.

c. the scientific method.

d. the empirical method.

_____ 5. Your roommate asks whether you believe that sunbathing can increase one's chances of getting skin cancer. You reply that of course it can because "baking in the sun is bound to be harmful to skin tissue." This belief was probably fixed by

a. the a priori method.

b. the method of authority.

c. the scientific method.

d. the method of tenacity.

_____ 6. Fixing belief a priori refers to

a. appealing to higher authorities.

b. believing views that seem reasonable.

c. believing opinions based on systematic observation.

d. believing only facts and not unsupported opinions.

_____ 7. A disadvantage of fixing beliefs by the method of authority or a priori is that

    a. neither method involves systematic observation.

    b. neither method offers a way of deciding which of two beliefs is superior to the other.

    c. neither method results in beliefs that are precise or testable.

    d. both a and b

_____ 8. The scientific method is the preferred technique for satisfying curiosity because it

    a. relies on systematic observation.

    b. is self-correcting.

    c. provides an empirical basis for fixing belief.

    d. all of the above

_____ 9. The _____ scientist emphasizes data and the _____ scientist emphasizes theory.

    a. inductive; deductive

    b. empirical; inductive

    c. deductive; inductive

    d. deductive; empirical

_____ 10. The inductive scientist

    a. conducts research in order to gain support for a particular theoretical view.

    b. believes that organized patterns of important empirical relations will emerge once enough data are collected.

    c. is not concerned with empirical observation.

    d. none of the above

_____ 11. The deductive scientist

    a. conducts research in order to gain support for a particular theoretical view.

    b. believes that organizational patterns will emerge once enough data are collected.

    c. is concerned primarily with empirical observation.

    d. none of the above

_____ 12. Which of the following is true concerning inductive and deductive scientists?

    a. Inductive scientists are more important because they provide basic data upon which to build theories.

    b. Deductive scientists are more important because they try to bring order out of the mass of data collected by empiricists.

    c. Most psychologists take either a purely inductive or purely deductive approach.

    d. none of the above

_____ 13. According to the falsifiability view of theories proposed by Popper, _____ in evaluating a theory.

a. negative evidence is more important than positive evidence

b. positive evidence is more important than negative evidence

c. replications of theories is most important

d. proving the unreliability of a theory is most important

_____ 14. One key aspect of the falsifiability view of theories is that falsifiability depends upon _____.

a. fabricating data

b. unreliable data

c. empirical observations

d. theoretical deductions

_____ 15. Which of the following procedures should, in the ideal case, yield one theory if the process is used repeatedly?

a. deductive reasoning

b. inductive reasoning

c. hypothesis testing

d. strong inference

_____ 16. Theories

       a. serve to organize existing data.

       b. generate predictions for situations where no data have yet been collected.

       c. can never be proven to be true.

       d. all of the above

_____ 17. Intervening variables serve to connect

       a. data and theory.

       b. hypothesis and experiment.

       c. independent and dependent variables.

       d. deduction and induction.

_____ 18. Inclusion of intervening variables may make a theory more

       a. precise.

       b. testable.

       c. parsimonious.

       d. valid.

_____ 19. Theories with mathematical formulations are said to be more _____ than verbal theories.

       a. parsimonious

       b. correct

       c. precise

       d. provable

_____ 20. If a theory is not _____ it can never be disproved.

    a. parsimonious

    b. precise

    c. testable

    d. mathematical

_____ 21. Which of the following is true?

    a. Data that are partially consistent with a theory can cause the theory to be modified.

    b. Data that are inconsistent with a theory can lead to the rejection of that theory.

    c. Data that are consistent with a theory can never prove the theory.

    d. All of the above.

_____ 22. A scientist theorizes that if all males were removed from society the incidence of violent crime would decrease by at least 80%. The major problem with this hypotheses is that it is not _____.

    a. precise

    b. testable

    c. parsimonious

    d. reliable

_____ 23. If a theory cannot be potentially disproved

    a. it is said to be unparsimonious.

    b. it is said to be testable.

    c. it is useless to scientists.

    d. none of the above

_____ 24. The fact that the relationship between basic psychological research and pressing social issues is not immediately obvious

    a. suggests that psychology has little to offer in the way of improving society.

    b. does not mean that no such relationship actually exists.

    c. means that federal funding should be withheld from psychological research.

    d. suggests that psychologists are studying the wrong problems.

_____ 25. Psychologists

    a. are more interested in physical situations that produce behavior rather than in the underlying process.

    b. are interested in neither physical situations nor underlying processes that produce behavior.

    c. are more interested in underlying processes that produce behavior than in physical situations.

    d. none of the above

TRUE-FALSE QUESTIONS

_____ 1. The method of authority involves taking someone else's word on faith.

_____ 2. Religious beliefs are generally formed by the method of tenacity.

_____ 3. An advantage of the scientific method over other methods of fixing beliefs is that it offers a means of determining the "superiority" of one belief over another.

_____ 4. Scientific data are necessarily empirical observations.

_____ 5. All approaches to science involve data and theory.

_____ 6. According to the inductive approach to science, general explanations are arrived at from a set of theoretical statements that can then be tested against data.

_____ 7. Theories induced from empirical observations are tentative due to the limited scope of our data.

_____ 8. Deductive approaches to science emphasize the primacy, or primary role, of theory.

_____ 9. Many correct predictions made by a theory can help to prove the theory to be correct.

_____ 10. A theory may never be proved.

_____ 11. The purposes of a psychological theory are to describe and explain behavior.

_____ 12. Intervening variables serve to link observables to non-observables.

_____ 13. Inclusion of intervening variables makes theories less parsimonious than they would otherwise be.

_____ 14. If two theories can account for the same data, but Theory A uses 10 statements and Theory B uses 15, then Theory B is the better theory.

_____ 15. One function of a scientific theory is to allow scientists to generate predictions for situations where no data have yet been obtained.

_____ 16. Verbal theories are generally considered useless in psychology.

_____ 17. The criterion of parsimony is most concerned with the number of findings a theory can account for.

_____ 18. A theory may be precise without being testable.

_____ 19. Applied research inevitably precedes basic research.

_____ 20. According to the text, the inability to predict which basic research being done today will have an impact on society years from now means that we should stop doing basic research.

_____ 21. Basic researchers generally assume that different mental processes occurs across different physical situations.

_____ 22. Establishing similar physical situations in which to observe behavior guarantees similarity in the mental processes underlying the behaviors.

ESSAY QUESTIONS

1. What are three methods for fixing belief? Which of these methods is superior to the others and why?

2. What are the advantages and disadvantages of the inductive and deductive approaches to science? Can either of these approaches be said to be the better of the two? Why or why not?

3. What is meant by basic research and applied research? Are the two endeavors related or separate enterprises?

4. What criteria may be used to evaluate theories? Which of these is the most crucial and why?

CHAPTER 3.
Observation in Psychological Research

SUMMARY

Psychology, as any science is based on observations. The quality of these observations, and the conditions under which they are made determine the conclusions we can draw from them. Useful scientific observations are truthful, that is, they are said to be valid. Experimental psychology is concerned with three types of validity.

Construct validity refers to the degree to which the independent and dependent variables in an experiment are accurate and appropriate reflections of the psychological processes that they represent. Construct validity is enhanced by employing operational definitions and protocols that specify how a behavior of interest is produced and precisely how it is to be measured.

External and internal validity refer to the kinds of conclusions that we are able to make from observations. Observations that are externally valid can be generalized to other settings and subject populations. External validity can be assessed by determining whether the same observations are made in replications of the original study conducted in different circumstances.

Internal validity refers to the ability to attribute causality to the relationship between variables. When several variables change at the same time, we are unable to conclude which caused the observed behavior to change.

There are several useful approaches to making observations in psychology. They include descriptive observations, relational observations, and experimental observations.

The descriptive observational approach is intended to describe behavior in a particular setting - what responses occur, and how often. Naturalistic observation, the case study, and the survey are examples of this descriptive approach. Descriptive research provides and extends the database for psychological research, and often serves as the precursor of more controlled experimentation. The limitations of the descriptive approach include an inability to evaluate the relationships among the observed events, the likely inability to reproduce the observations, especially in the case study, and the difficulty of maintaining descriptive objectivity and avoiding anthropomorphism.

Relational observation is aimed at discovering how two or more variables are related to each other. This relationship is measured by a correlation coefficient, which tells us the degree to which we can successfully predict one variable if we know the value of the other. To obtain a useful measure of correlation it is necessary to ensure that a wide range of each variable is included in the sample; a truncated range of either variable results in an artificially low measure of the strength of the relationship. Caution should be used in interpreting correlations. It is generally inappropriate to attribute causality on the basis of correlational evidence alone, since the correlation coefficient cannot identify which of two related variables is causal, or whether both measured variables are effects of an unmeasured cause. A variation of the correlational approach, the cross-lagged-panel correlation procedure, provides better evidence of causal relationships.

In principle, experimentation provides internal validity, that is, it allows us to infer a causal relationship between the independent and dependent variables. This is because the independent variable is manipulated while the effects of other variables are controlled. If the dependent variable is altered under these conditions, we can conclude that the manipulation of the independent variable was the proximal cause of this behavioral effect.

KEY TERMS

anthropomorphizing	naturalistic observations
case study	operational definitions
construct validity	Pearson's product-moment correlation
correlation coefficient	protocols
crossed-lagged-panel procedure	proximate causes
descriptive observations	relational observations
deviant-case analysis	replication
ethogram	scatter diagrams
explanation	surveys
ex post facto	truncated range
external validity	ultimate causes
internal validity	validity

PROGRAMMED REVIEW

1. The _____ of an observation refers to its truth.

2. _____ validity refers to the extent that a variable is an appropriate and accurate measure of whatever the variable represents.

3. _____ and _____ _____ are possible threats to construct validity.

4. An _____ _____ is a recipe that specifies how a construct is produced and measured in an experiment. Use of these helps to minimize _____ invalidity.

5. A _____ is a precise specification of how the measurement of behavior is to be undertaken.

6. _____ validity refers to the extent that research can be generalized to other settings and subject populations.

7. If we wanted to demonstrate that findings of a particular experiment had external validity, we should _____ the study under altered conditions.

8. The ability to claim that changes in behavior are caused by manipulation of the independent variable refers to _____ _____.

9. The major threat to internal validity is _____.

10. _____ observations enumerate what behaviors occur and in what quantity and frequency.

11. Examples of descriptive observations include _____ _____, the _____ _____ and _____.

12. Descriptive observations are a useful first step in research since they provide and extend the _____ that can lead to more controlled experimentation.

13. Descriptive observations alone can not tell us how events are _____ to each other.

14. Descriptive observation, in particular the case study, is limited because the observations often can not be _____.

15. It is difficult to maintain a descriptive rather than interpretative level of observation, for example, avoiding _____, the attribution of human characteristics to animals.

16. Relational research uses a _____ _____ to indicate the degree of relationship between two variables.

17. If two variables are related, we can use knowledge of one variable to _____ the other.

18.   Most measures of correlation range in value from _____ to _____ .

19.   The larger the absolute value of the correlation coefficient, the _____ the relationship.

20.   The sign of the correlation coefficient tells us the _____ of the relationship between two variables.

21.   A _____ _____ is a kind of graph commonly used to present correlational data.

22.   We are not entitled to infer a _____ relationship between two variables, solely on the basis of correlational evidence.

23.   The reason that variable A is correlated with variable B might be that A is the cause of B, B is the cause of A, or that both A and B are caused by an unknown _____ _____ .

24.   Correlation coefficients may be artificially _____ if the range of either variable is restricted.

25.   The use of the _____-_____-_____ correlational procedure provides greater internal validity than is provided by the traditional correlational approach.

26.   In principle, _____ observation allows us to infer causality, because by manipulating the independent variable, and holding other variables constant, we know the direction of the effect.

EXPERIMENTAL PROJECT

        Some psychologists have suggested that there may be a relationship between birth order and intelligence, with first-born children being more intelligent than their younger siblings. In fact, it has been shown that intelligence scores decline steadily with birth order. You can test this hypothesis in the following way. Obtain the number of older siblings that a person has, and let this be the X score. Then let that person's grade point average be his or her Y score. (We are assuming that grade point average is an indicant of intelligence.) Obtain these same measurements from several individuals. You may query as few as 10 people, but it is preferable to have a larger sample size (n) of 25 or so. You might want to pool your data with that collected by other members of the class. Correlate the scores using the Pearson correlation formula found in the text. If the hypothesis is correct, you should obtain a negative correlation with grade point average decreasing as the number of older siblings increases. Do your results support the hypothesis? If not, what reasons can you offer for the discrepancy? What are the implications of your findings?

EXPERIMENTAL DILEMMAS

1.   An industrial psychologist interested in the effects of a work training program on job performance reported the following study. Fifty garment factory workers were given on the job training in a program that lasted either one or two weeks. Afterward their performance in terms of number of work pieces completed in one day was correlated with the number of weeks spent in training. The Pearson coefficient obtained between these two measures was -.02. From this result the researcher concluded that the work training program was ineffective and should be abandoned. If you were a top management executive, would you comply with the researcher's suggestion? If not, why?

2.   A social psychologist interested in the effects of unemployment on alcohol abuse conducted the following study. She mailed questionnaires to the homes of workers who had been laid off from a local automobile plant. The questionnaires were mailed at various time intervals and the workers were asked to fill them out anonymously and to return them. Fifty percent of the questionnaires were completed and returned. For those

individuals who returned the questionnaires, the correlation between alcohol consumption and length of unemployment was found to be +.64. That is, more alcohol was consumed as the period of unemployment progressed. In her report the researcher stated that "the conditions of unemployment produce a tendency for people to increase their alcohol intake." If you were the editor in charge of deciding whether this work would be accepted for publication, what would your judgement be?

MULTIPLE CHOICE QUESTIONS

_____ 1. We have confidence that our psychological descriptions, relationships, and explanations are good when they are based on
   a. testable hypotheses.
   b. valid observations.
   c. useful research.
   d. all of the above

_____ 2. The degree to which independent and dependent variables accurately reflect or measure what they are intended to measure is
   a. construct validity.
   b. external validity.
   c. interval validity.
   d. predictive validity.

_____ 3. If a subject were apprehensive about being in an experiment, it is likely that time to read a passage would lack _____ _____ as a measure of reading skill.
   a. construct validity
   b. external validity
   c. interval validity
   d. predictive validity

_____ 4. A specification of the conditions that would be used to produce anxiety in experimental subjects, and of the way that this anxiety would be measured, constitute a _____ of anxiety.

    a. external validation procedure

    b. interval validation procedure

    c. operational definition

    d. protocol

_____ 5. The use of protocols and operational definitions is useful in reducing _____ invalidity.

    a. construct

    b. external

    c. interval

    d. predictive

_____ 6. The extent to which research findings can be generalized to other populations and settings refers to

    a. construct validity.

    b. external validity.

    c. interval validity.

    d. predictive validity.

_____ 7. Replicating experiments using different tasks, different experimental settings, or with different subject populations helps to establish

    a. construct validity.

    b. external validity.

    c. interval validity.

    d. predictive validity.

_____ 8. Whether or not we can claim that changes in the independent variable caused changes to occur in the dependent variable refers to

    a. construct validity.

    b. external validity.

    c. interval validity.

    d. predictive validity.

_____ 9. Confounding in an experiment threatens
   a. construct validity.
   b. external validity.
   c. interval validity.
   d. two of the above

_____ 10. The advantage of descriptive observation is that
   a. it allows for a good deal of experimental control.
   b. it allows for easy replication.
   c. it helps to define a problem area and raise interesting questions.
   d. it is primarily concerned with relationships.

_____ 11. A relatively complete inventory of specific behaviors performed by one species of animal, and that is useful in naturalistic observation is a
   a. ethogram.
   b. response catalog.
   c. survey.
   d. protocol.

_____ 12. An intensive investigation of a particular person, or a particular group of people is called
   a. a case study.
   b. an ethogram.
   c. relational research.
   d. a survey.

_____ 13. In a deviant-case analysis, the researcher
   a. conducts an intensive investigation of an unusual individual.
   b. conducts naturalistic observations in an environment populated by deviants.
   c. investigates the relationships of an unusual person.
   d. considers two cases with many similarities but that differ in the outcome.

_____ 14. When you brought a new puppy home, your old dog Spot bit you on the ankle. Calling Spot 'jealous' is an example of

    a. anthropomorphism.

    b. a deviant-case study.

    c. naturalistic observation.

    d. concept validity.

_____ 15. The primary problem unique to descriptive observation is that it

    a. does not allow us to assess the relations among events.

    b. suffers from external invalidity.

    c. is only concerned with deviant cases.

    d. can not be quantified.

_____ 16. The use of correlational techniques permits the researcher to

    a. make predictions on the basis of the obtained results.

    b. understand why two variables are related.

    c. manipulate the effect of one variable on another.

    d. infer a lack of causation.

_____ 17. Which of the following reflects a positive correlation?

    a. The ratio of head size to height decreases with age.

    b. Yearly income increases as educational level is increased.

    c. Men own more cars than women.

    d. Amount of exercise is inversely related to rate of heart attacks.

_____ 18. The cross-lagged-panel correlation is used to

    a. examine multiple correlations.

    b. partial out irrelevant variables.

    c. examine patterns of correlations over time.

    d. all of the above

_____ 19. When we have conducted a proper experiment, we can conclude that the changes in the independent variable were the _____ cause of the change in behavior.
a. real
b. ultimate
c. proximate
d. all of the above

TRUE-FALSE QUESTIONS

_____ 1. Validity and invalidity refer to the best approximation to the truth or falsity of propositions.

_____ 2. Amount of hair, as a measure of intelligence, would seem to lack external validity.

_____ 3. Random error is a major threat to the interval validity of an observation.

_____ 4. Protocols are more precise than operational definitions.

_____ 5. Research findings that are only true of a particular strain of white rats would seem to lack predictive validity.

_____ 6. Construct validity can be demonstrated by replicating an experiment with different tasks.

_____ 7. In principle, experimental observations permit causal statements.

_____ 8. Imprecise protocols are the major threat to internal validity.

_____ 9. Naturalistic observation is inherently unsystematic in the way that data is collected.

_____ 10. The text suggests than descriptive observation is not inferior to, but simply prior to experimentation.

_____ 11. Ethology refers to the study of naturally occurring behavior (often in the wild).

_____ 12. Eibl-Eibesfeldt's research on the eyebrow flash is a good use of the survey technique.

_____ 13. Lovelace and Twohig used a survey to demonstrate that younger and older people used different strategies to remember things.

_____ 14. While external validity may be questionable, descriptive observation guarantees internal and construct validity.

_____ 15. Correlation coefficients usually range from 0.0 to 1.0.

_____ 16. Positive values of the correlation coefficient indicate stronger relationships than negative values.

_____ 17. A low correlation between variables A and B is proof that neither variable caused the other.

_____ 18. If an unknown third variable caused both variables A and B, the correlation coefficient would be smaller than if A caused B or vice versa.

_____ 19. Psychology, as all sciences, is concerned with demonstrating ultimate causes for the events in the real world.

ESSAY QUESTIONS

1. Discuss how confounding can reduce both construct and interval validity.

2. Discuss the relationship between causation and correlation.

3. What additional power is provided by a deviant-case study over an ordinary case study? By a cross-lagged-panel correlation procedure over more traditional correlational approaches?

CHAPTER 4.

Measurement in Psychological Research

SUMMARY

Measurement is a systematic way of assigning numbers to objects and their attributes. Psychologists use four types of measurement scales which have different properties. The nominal scale, in which numbers are used as names to identify objects, measures just the property of difference. The ordinal scale measures differences in magnitude; larger numbers are assigned to objects with a greater amount of whatever is being measured. Interval scales, in addition to measuring differences in magnitudes, have the property of equal units, which mean that these measurement can be added and subtracted. In addition to all these properties, ratio scales have the property of a true zero point, which means that it is meaningful to say that one measurement is twice (or half) as large as another measurement. The type of measurement scale used determines the kind of statistical analysis that is appropriate for a set of data, and it affects the conclusions that can be drawn from that data.

In order for the data from a research project to be useful, these data must be both reliable and valid. Reliability refers to the consistency of a measurement or observation. The reliability of psychological tests is determined by comparing the test scores of the same group of people who take the test on two different occasions (test-retest and parallel form reliability) and by comparing the scores obtained on one half of the items with those obtained on the other half (split-half reliability).

Reliability and validity in experimentation involves several factors. One concern is with the statistical reliability of the results which is determined by inferential statistics. We can be more sure of experimental results when they are based on large samples, since the power of statistical tests to detect effects increases with the sample size. A valid sample is one that reflects the characteristics of the population it represents. Large samples are more representative than small samples, and random sampling from the population increases the likelihood of obtaining a valid sample. Random assignment of subjects to the experimental conditions reduces the possibility of confounding treatments with individual characteristics. Finally, experimental reliability is most convincingly demonstrated by replicating an experiment.

One of the oldest forms of measurement in psychology is referred to as psychophysics, measuring sensations that arise from physical stimulation. The text describes the use of a psychophysical method, the method of limits, to measure absolute thresholds, the smallest stimulus intensity that is reliably detected, and the difference threshold, the smallest difference in intensity between two stimuli that is reliably detected.

Weber found that the size of the difference threshold relative to the standard was approximately constant for a specific sensory modality. Based largely on this finding, Fechner developed a psychophysical law that stated that the magnitude of sensation is proportional to the logarithm of the stimulus intensity. The evidence supporting Fechner's law was based on an indirect scaling method. Fechner's findings were called into question by Stevens who stated that the magnitude of sensation was a power function of the stimulus intensity. Stevens' law is supported by a direct scaling technique called magnitude estimation.

When data are presented in a figure or a table, it is important to read the title of the table or figure, as well as the heading of tables and the axes of figures. In figures, the dependent variable is plotted on the Y axis, or ordinate, while the independent variable is plotted on the X axis, or abscissa. The appearance of a graph is greatly influenced by the scale of the ordinate.

KEY TERMS

abscissa

absolute threshold

difference

difference threshold

direct scaling

equal interval

experimental reliability

Fechner's law

indirect scaling

interval of uncertainty

interval scale

just-noticeable difference (JND)

magnitude

magnitude estimation

measurement

method of limits

nominal scale

ordinal scale

ordinate

parallel forms

point of subjective equality

population

power

predictive validity

psychophysical methods

psychophysics

random assignment

random sampling

ratio scale

reliability

sample

split-half reliability

staircase method

statistical reliability

Stevens' law

test-retest reliability

threshold

true zero

Weber's law

PROGRAMMED REVIEW

1. _____ refers to a systematic way of assigning numbers or names to objects and their attributes.

2. The measurement scale that assigns names or numbers solely on the basis of differences among objects is the _____ scale.

3. If a measurement scale can reflect that some objects have more of a certain attribute than other objects, then the measurement scale has the property of _____. The least informative scale with this property is the _____ scale.

4. The Fahrenheit and Centigrade temperature scales are examples of _____ measurement scales because they have _____ _____.

5. Length, height, and weight are measured with _____ scales of measurement, since in addition to having equal units, they also have the property of a _____ _____.

6. Most psychological measurement is at the level of _____ or _____ scales.

7. _____ refers to the consistency of measures.

8. The procedure of giving the same test twice in succession over a short time interval is used to determine the _____ - _____ reliability of the test.

9. The form of test reliability determined by administering a single test and looking at the correlations among different sets of items is known as _____ - _____ reliability.

10. _____ statistics are used to determine whether an experimental effect is due to the manipulation of the independent variable, that is, whether the effect is _____ _____.

11. The ability of a statistical test to detect experimental effects, that is, its _____, is increased by _____ the size of the experimental sample.

12. A sampling procedure in which every member of the population has an equal chance of being selected is called a _____ sampling procedure.

13. One way of increasing the representativeness of a sample is to _____ the size of the sample.

14. Replication of research is the scientist's best strategy in establishing _____ reliability.

15. Psychophysics refers to measuring judgements of stimuli that vary along a known _____ dimension.

16. The method of limits is a _____ _____ developed by Gustav Fechner that can be used to measure both absolute and difference _____.

17. Using the method of limits, the mean of the points in each trial block where the observed switches from Yes to No is called the _____ _____.

18. _____ thresholds are based upon _____ judgements, where an unchanging comparison stimulus is judged relative to a series of _____ stimuli.

19. The difference between the upper threshold and the lower threshold is called the _____ of _____.

20. The arithmetic mean of the upper and lower thresholds is called the _____ of _____ _____.

21. Weber found that the size of the difference threshold relative to the intensity of the standard stimulus is _____.

22. One difference between the traditional method of limits and the staircase method is that the staircase method concentrates responses around the _____.

23. Fechner's law relates the magnitude of sensation to the stimulus _____. The magnitude of sensation is taken to be the number of _____-_____ _____ a stimulus lies above the absolute threshold.

24. According to Fechner's law, sensation magnitude is a function of the _____ of the stimulus intensity.

25. Fechner measured sensation magnitude _____, while S.S. Stevens measured it _____, using the method of _____ _____.

26. According to Stevens' law, the magnitude of sensation is a _____ function of the stimulus intensity.

27. The vertical axis in a figure is called the _____ and the horizontal axis is called the _____.

28. In figures, the _____ variable is generally plotted on the abscissa.

29. A bar graph might be used if the independent variable was measured at the _____ level.

EXPERIMENTAL PROJECT

How good are we at estimating the number of cards in a stack by feeling the thickness of the stack? How does the psychological experience of thickness change with the number of cards in the stack?

Get about 400 3x5 index cards, and make stacks of varying numbers of cards. It's a good idea to make each stack about twice as large as the next smaller stack. So if your smallest stack was 3 cards, the other stacks would have 6, 12, 24, 48, 96, and 192 cards.

Arrange the stacks in a random order, and present them one at a time to a blindfolded subject. Record the subject's estimate of the number of cards in each stack, based on his or her feeling the thickness of the stack. Repeat this procedure about four times (with different random presentations) for each subject, and average the estimates for each stack size. Collect data from 3 or 4 subjects in this manner.

A convenient way to look at these data is by preparing a couple of graphs. One of the graphs should show the estimates on the ordinate, and the <u>log</u> of the number of cards on the abscissa. (A convenient way to do this is to plot the actual values on semi-log graph paper, which should be available at the campus supply store. If this paper is not available, use ordinary graph paper, and plot the logs of the various stack sizes on the abscissa.) If Fechner's law holds for these data, the points on the graph should fall on a straight line, since sensation (the estimated number of cards) is a function of the log of the stimulus intensity (the actual number of cards). The slope of this line should be the same for each subject.

The other graph will be used to evaluate Steven's law for these data. This time we want to plot the <u>log</u> of the estimates on the ordinate, and the <u>log</u> of the stack size on the abscissa. (So, ask for log-log graph paper.) If Stevens' law holds, the points on this second graph should fall on a straight line. The slope of this line will be equal to the <u>power</u> to which stimulus intensity must be raised to reflect sensation magnitude.

Which psychophysical law receives greater support? Are all the subjects similar to each other in the patterns of their judgements? On the basis of your work, can you predict the estimated number of cards that would be reported if you gave your subjects all 400 cards to feel?

EXPERIMENTAL DILEMMA

As discussed in the textbook, in order for a measurement technique to be useful as a scientific tool it is essential that the technique be reliable. A seven category rating scale for measuring friendliness was devised and administered to a sample of 15-20 people who all rated the same individuals. One week later the same scale was administered to the same sample of people.

It was found that the two sets of scores were not identical. Some people who were rated as very friendly on the first administration were rated as unfriendly a week later. Does this mean that the rating scale is an unreliable measurement technique? Is there a more appropriate way in which to measure the reliability of the rating scale? Is it possible that the rating scale is a reliable tool but the reason for the test-retest results are that peoples' perceptions of the rated individual may have changed over the one week interval?

MULTIPLE CHOICE QUESTIONS

_____ 1. Which of the following is <u>not</u> one of the types of measurement scales that psychologists are most concerned with?

  a. interval
  b. nominal
  c. ordinal
  d. psychometric
  e. ratio

_____ 2. The scale of measurement that has the most stringent requirements is the _____ scale.

  a. interval
  b. nominal
  c. ordinal
  d. ratio

_____ 3. The Kelvin scale of temperature is an example of a(n) _____ scale.

  a. interval
  b. nominal
  c. ordinal
  d. ratio

_____ 4. The numbers on an athlete's jersey are an example of a(n) _____ scale.

   a. interval

   b. nominal

   c. ordinal

   d. ratio

_____ 5. At a horse race the finishing positions are determined by how fast each horse ran the race. Thus, the first finishing horse ran the fastest, the second place horse ran the next fastest, and so on. These finishing positions numbers (i.e., First, Second,...) form a(n) _____ scale.

   a. interval

   b. nominal

   c. ordinal

   d. ratio

_____ 6. When we say that a measure of behavior is reliable, we mean that it is

   a. appropriate.

   b. consistent.

   c. experimental.

   d. useful.

_____ 7. A result is said to be statistically reliable if

   a. the result is replicated under conditions that are very different from those of the original experiment.

   b. the number of observations per experimental condition is high.

   c. it is very unlikely that the result occurred by chance.

   d. operational definitions are used to define the dependent variable.

_____ 8. The entire set of potential participants is called the
_____. The portion of all individuals tested is
called a _____ of subjects.
   a. population; sample
   b. sample; population
   c. subject pool; random sample
   d. population; population subset

_____ 9. Random sampling is done to
   a. increase statistical reliability.
   b. increase sample representativeness.
   c. minimize confounding.
   d. two of the above

_____10. Random assignment is done to
   a. increase statistical reliability.
   b. increase sample representativeness.
   c. minimize confounding.
   d. two of the above

_____11. The greater the number of observations upon which a
sample statistic is based,
   a. the greater the reliability of the statistic.
   b. the greater the variability of the statistic.
   c. the greater the error component of the statistic.
   d. none of the above

_____12. "One replication is worth a thousand t-tests." This
adage implies that _____ is more important than
_____.
   a. experimental reliability; statistical reliability
   b. validity; reliability
   c. retest reliability; test reliability
   d. experimental reliability; test reliability

_____13. The determination of psychological reaction to events that lie along a physical dimension is called
a. experimentation.
b. measurement.
c. psychophysics.
d. scaling.

_____14. The smallest stimulus intensity that can be detected is called the
a. absolute threshold.
b. difference threshold.
c. just-noticeable difference.
d. minimal stimulus.

_____15. The method of limits is a technique used to determine the
a. stimulus intensity.
b. stimulus quality.
c. stimulus duration.
d. threshold.

_____16. The method of limits involves
a. beginning each block of trials with a stimulus intensity that can be clearly perceived.
b. beginning each block of trials with a stimulus intensity too low to be perceived.
c. alternating each block of trials between a and b above.
d. either a or b, but not both

_____17. A threshold based on an observer's ability to detect a single stimulus is called the
a. difference threshold.
b. absolute threshold.
c. mean threshold.
d. interval uncertainty.

_____18. In a task where the observer compares the weight of a constant comparison stimulus with the weights of a changing stimulus using the method of limits, the point of subjective equality is operationally defined as
   a. the mean of the stimulus values corresponding to the last "heavier" response and the first "equal" response.
   b. the mean of the stimulus values corresponding to the last "equal" response and the first "lighter" response.
   c. the difference between the upper and lower thresholds.
   d. the mean of a and b above

_____19. The mean of the upper and lower difference thresholds is called the
   a. absolute threshold.
   b. interval of uncertainty.
   c. point of subjective equality.
   d. standard stimulus.

_____20. According to Weber's law, the size of the difference threshold relative to the standard stimulus is constant for a particular
   a. person.
   b. sensory modality.
   c. stimulus intensity.
   d. all of the above

_____21. Fechner believed that sensation magnitude could be measured in units of
   a. physical intensity.
   b. just-noticeable differences.
   c. sensory modality.
   d. absolute threshold.

_____22. Fechner measured sensation _____, and found that sensation was a _____ function of stimulus intensity.

a. directly; log

b. directly; power

c. indirectly; log

d. indirectly; power

_____23. Stevens used _____ to measure sensation magnitude.

a. indirect scaling

b. magnitude estimation

c. the method of limits

d. the staircase method

_____24. According to the text, Fechner measured sensation magnitude at the _____ level, and Stevens measured it at the _____ level.

a. ordinal; ordinal

b. ordinal; ratio

c. ratio; ordinal

d. ratio; ratio

_____25. In a figure the vertical axis is called the _____ and the _____ variable is generally on this axis.

a. ordinate; independent

b. ordinate; dependent

c. abscissa; independent

d. abscissa; dependent

TRUE-FALSE QUESTIONS

_____ 1. A ratio scale has a true zero point.

_____ 2. A nominal scale uses names instead of numbers.

_____ 3. An ordinal scale has only the scale properties of differences and magnitude.

_____ 4. An interval scale is the weakest type of measurement scale.

_____ 5. If we measure the same thing on several occasions and obtain about the same numbers, we can conclude that our measuring technique is reliable.

_____ 6. Split-half reliability involves splitting the sample of subjects into two separate groups and seeing if there is a significant difference between the two groups.

_____ 7. Inferential statistics are used to determine the validity of a set of data.

_____ 8. Increasing the number of observations we make helps increase the reliability of our results.

_____ 9. Random assignment refers to randomly assigning subjects to treatment conditions.

_____10. In general, experimental reliability is preferred over statistical reliability.

_____11. Psychophysical methods are techniques used by psychologists to attempt to relate psychological judgement to the characteristics of physical stimuli.

_____12. Absolute thresholds are based upon relative judgements where a constant comparison stimulus is judged relative to a series of changing stimuli.

_____13. Using the method of limits, the alternating blocks of increasing and decreasing trials must each start at the same intensity.

_____14. The mean of an upper and lower threshold is called the interval of uncertainty.

_____15. The version of the method of limits called the staircase method is efficient because it concentrates responses around the threshold.

_____16. In order to develop his psychophysical law, Fechner found it necessary to disprove Weber's law.

_____17. The method of magnitude estimation yields a ratio scale.

_____18. In a figure the horizontal axis is called the abscissa.

_____19. A bar graph is typically used to present data when the levels of the independent variable are defined at the ratio level.

_____20. If the measurement of the dependent variable is of a high enough level, it is impossible to change the appearance of a figure.

ESSAY QUESTIONS

1. Averages are easy to calculate, and are often used in situations where they shouldn't be used. Consider your academic grades, and the common overall measure of academic performance, the grade-point average. What assumptions about the quality of measurement are made when a grade-point average is determined? Are these assumptions reasonable? How do you think the valedictorian should be selected?

2. What is the staircase method of establishing thresholds and how does this method differ from the method of limits?

CHAPTER 5.
Basics of Experimentation

SUMMARY

John Stuart Mill argued that causation can be inferred if (a) some result follows an event, (b) the result and the event vary together, and (c) it can be shown that the event produces the result. These three conditions are met when the joint method of agreement and difference are used.

Experiments employ three types of variables: independent variables, which are the factors that are manipulated or varied by the experimenter; dependent variables, which are the objects or events that are observed and measured; and control variables, which are those aspects of the experiment that the researcher holds constant. To avoid null results (i.e., the failure of the independent variable to control behavior) it is important that the researcher select appropriate levels of the independent variable. It is also essential that the dependent variable produce reliable data and that the experimental conditions effectively control for (or assess the effects of) extraneous variation. Finally, it is important that the experimental conditions do not produce performance levels that are restricted to either the upper or the lower limit of the dependent variable.

Researchers often employ more than one independent variable within a single experiment. This is done to increase efficiency in the research process, to ensure that the effects produced by one independent variable are not restricted to only one set of experimental conditions (i.e., that the results generalize), and to determine whether the effects produced by one independent variable are the same or different across the levels of other independent variables. Researchers sometimes also employ more than one dependent variable in an experiment. This serves to provide additional information and to increase the generality of the results of the experiment.

KEY TERMS

ceiling effect	ex post facto
confounding	floor effect
control	independent variable
control group	interaction
control variable	joint method of agreement
dependent variable	and difference
experiment	null results
experimental group	type 2 error

PROGRAMMED REVIEW

1. The experiment of Brennen et al. was designed to determine whether _____ or _____ was more important in relieving the tip-of-the-tongue state.

2. An experiment (such as Brennen's study) is designed to allow the researcher to find the _____ of a behavioral event.

3. The method of observation that asserts that "Result R always follows Event E, if E and R vary together and Event E produces Result R" is known as the _____.

4. Control in experimentation can come about in three different ways:
   (a) there is a control condition (or group) for purposes of _____ ;
   (b) we can produce different levels of the _____ variables;
   (c) we can control the _____ _____ and keep these factors constant.

5. Experiments employ three types of variables:
   (a) the variable that is manipulated or varied is the _____ variable;
   (b) the events or behaviors that are observed and measured are the _____ variables;
   (c) those aspects of the experiment that the researcher holds constant are called the _____ variables.

6. Those subjects that receive the independent variable are referred to collectively as the _____ group.

7. The control group is comprised of subjects who do not receive the _____ variable.

8. The major drawback in an ex post facto research project is that the researcher loses experimental _____ .

9. When we select an independent variable we do so because we believe it will _____ behavior.

10. A failure of the independent variable to control behavior is sometimes referred to as a _____ _____ .

11. If an independent variable is not an important factor in affecting behavior, then an experiment that employs this variable may produce _____ _____ .

12. A failure to produce a strong manipulation of the _____ variable may lead to null results.

13. In order for a dependent variable to be useful it is important that the variable produces _____ data.

14. An unreliable dependent variable can often produce _____ results.

15. If performance levels (as measured by the dependent variable) are at the bottom of the measurement scale then this can result in a _____ effect. If performance levels are at the top of the scale then this can result in a _____ effect.

16. It is especially important to control extraneous factors when the magnitude of the effect produced by the independent variable is relatively _____.

17. The most direct experimental technique for controlling extraneous variation is to hold the variable(s) _____.

18. The likelihood of committing a Type 2 error (increases/decreases) _____ as we lower the level of statistical significance.

19. It is (more/less) _____ efficient to conduct an experiment with three independent variables than to conduct three separate experiments.

20. If the same results are obtained across several independent variables than these results are said to be _____.

21. If the effects produced by one independent variable are not the same across the levels of a second independent variable this result is termed a(n) _____.

22. Piliavin, Piliavin, and Rodin (1975) conducted an experiment to discover when a bystander would help in an emergency. The independent variables were:
    (a)_____
    (b)_____

23. In an experiment employing only one independent variable it is not possible to obtain _____ effects.

24. In an experiment employing more than one dependent variable the results must be analyzed using _____ statistical procedures.

25.   Typically   only   _____   or   _____   dependent
       variables are used in a single experiment.

EXPERIMENTAL PROJECT

    As part of a project in an environmental psychology class you
are given the following assignment: Determine whether it is
possible to "defend" a table in the library by preventing anyone
else from sitting down at the table with you.

    How would you conduct an experiment to answer this question?
What is the hypothesis you want to test? After you have
formulated a testable hypothesis, design an experiment to test
this hypothesis, then identify the independent, dependent, and
control variables.

    Now that you have designed your experiment you might want to
actually conduct the experiment. However, check with your
instructor before you run off to the library: most colleges and
universities have regulations concerning research involving
human participants. There may be ethical reasons why you can
not or should not perform your experiment. (See Chapter 12 for
a discussion of ethics in psychological research.)

EXPERIMENTAL DILEMMA

    Male college students are recruited to participate in a motor
learning experiment. The task being used required the subjects
to throw a dart at a one inch diameter target mounted on a wall
10 feet from the subject. The researcher was interested in the
effects of monetary incentives on learning this task. All
subjects were first given 10 practice throws before the
experiment began. Subjects in the high-incentive group were
told they would receive 10 cents for every successful throw.
Subjects in the low-incentive group were offered 5 cents for
each successful throw. Subjects in both groups were also told
that they would receive $3.50 just for participating in the
experiment, in addition to the payments for successful throws.

Subjects were assigned to the two groups at random. All subjects were given 50 throws. The results showed that there was no significant difference between the two groups in terms of the number of successful throws. The researcher concluded that monetary incentives have no effect on performance in this type of task.

Would you accept this conclusion? Are there any additional data that would allow you to answer this question more confidently?

MULTIPLE CHOICE QUESTIONS

_____ 1. In Brennen's experiments on the tip-of-the-tongue (TOT) state, the independent variable was _____ and the dependent variable was _____.
a. the cuing condition; percent of pictures identified
b. the cuing condition; percent of TOTs resolved
c. sex of the celebrity; percent of pictures identified
d. sex of the celebrity; percent of TOTs resolved

_____ 2. We can use John Stuart Mills joint method of agreement and difference to decide that cuing with initials caused an increase in TOT resolutions because
a. with initials there was increased resolution.
b. without initials there was no increased resolution.
c. both a and b
d. neither a nor b

_____ 3. The hallmark of an experiment is
a. repeated positive correlations.
b. repeated significant effects.
c. producing a comparison by controlling the occurrence/nonoccurrence of a variable and observing the outcome.
d. random assignment of subjects to conditions and tight procedural control over variables.

_____ 4. If two variables occur together in nature, then there is no control over the presumed cause. As a result this observation reveals:

a. correlations.

b. causal relations.

c. descriptive data.

d. unreliable data.

e. only strong relations.

_____ 5. In an experiment, the variable manipulated by the experimenter is the _____ variable and the behavior recorded by the experimenter is the _____ variable.

a. independent; dependent

b. dependent; independent

c. observed; control

d. control; observed

_____ 6. Dependent variables are dependent upon

a. experimental manipulations.

b. behavior of the subject.

c. experimental control.

d. comparisons produced experimentally.

e. being held constant.

_____ 7. The variable manipulated by the experimenter in order to study its effect on behavior is called the

a. control variable.

b. experimental variable.

c. dependent variable.

d. independent variable.

_____ 8. In principle, experiments are designed to allow the researcher to make statements about

a. causation.

b. contiguity.

c. correlation.

d. strength of relations.

e. both b and c

_____ 9. Null results can be caused by problems associated with the _____ variable(s).

    a. control

    b. experimental

    c. independent

    d. dependent

    e. both c and d

_____10. A good dependent variable should be

    a. reliable.

    b. related to the independent variable.

    c. of theoretical interest.

    d. easy to observe.

_____11. Floor effects and ceiling effects result from using

    a. an unreliable dependent variable.

    b. only one level of the independent variable.

    c. two very extreme levels of the independent variable.

    d. a restricted range of the dependent variable.

_____12. A control variable is

    a. a potential dependent variable that is held constant.

    b. a potential independent variable that is held constant.

    c. a dependent variable that is varied in a controlled fashion by the experimenter.

    d. an independent variable that is varied in a controlled fashion by the experimenter.

_____13. Which of the following is <u>not</u> an advantage of manipulating several independent variables within the same experiment, as opposed to manipulating these variables in separate experiments?

a. greater efficiency

b. interaction effects may be observed

c. control variables are more likely to be held constant

d. results are easier to interpret

_____14. Which of the following is <u>not</u> one of the ways that control is used in an experiment?

a. The control group is used as a basis of comparison.

b. The independent variable is under controlled manipulation.

c. The independent variable is directly controlled by the researcher.

d. Extraneous variables are controlled by being held constant.

e. All of the above represent ways in which control is used.

_____15. The "control" in control variable refers to

a. the influence exerted on behavior.

b. the fact that the experimenter must control the variable to ensure a valid comparison.

c. the fact that the control group experiences the variable.

d. the fact that the variable is subject to controlled manipulation in the experiment.

e. the fact that the variable is under the direct control of the subject.

_____16. An interaction occurs when

    a. the effects produced by one independent variable are not the same at each level of a second independent variable.

    b. the effects produced by one level of an independent variable are not the same at other levels of that independent variable.

    c. the effects produced by an independent variable are not the same at each level of the dependent variable.

    d. the effects produced by a dependent variable are not the same at each level of the independent variable.

_____17. A valid experiment may produce null results because:

    a. the levels of the independent variable are too similar to each other.

    b. the dependent variable is subject to a ceiling effect.

    c. extraneous variables are not held constant.

    d. all of the above

    e. both a and b

_____18. Which of the following fictional results is <u>not</u> an example of an interaction?

    a. with normally active children, the stimulating effect of amphetamines increases as the dosage increases, but with hyperactive children the greater the dosage of amphetamines, the calmer the children

    b. the level of humidity greatly affects people's comfort levels in the summer heat, but in the winter cold humidity levels make much less of a difference on comfort levels

    c. people who attend church regularly donate more money to charity than nonchurchgoers unless they are poor, in which case church attendance makes no difference

    d. children who watch violent TV shows are more aggressive than children who do not watch violent TV shows, although all children watch the same amount of TV

    e. college men go out drinking more often than college women, unless they are poor, in which case women go out drinking more often

_____19. The nature of the interaction in the study by Piliavin, Piliavin and Rodin was

    a. presence or absence of the intern had little effect if the victim had no birthmark but a large effect if the victim had a birthmark.

    b. presence or absence of an intern was more important than presence or absence of a birthmark.

    c. presence or absence of a birthmark was more important than presence or absence of an intern.

    d. the presence or absence of a birthmark had a larger effect when the intern was present than when the intern was not present.

    e. both a and b

TRUE-FALSE QUESTIONS

_____ 1. Graessle et al found that rats given prenatal decompressions began to climb at a later age, and gained weight more slowly than controls.

_____ 2. The joint method of agreement and difference asserts that if a series of observations all agree on a specific ordering of two events than the first event must have caused the second event.

_____ 3. The joint method of agreement and difference requires pairs of observations made at the same time by the different observers.

_____ 4. The sole difference between the experimental group and the control group is that the former receives the independent variable whereas the later does not receive this variable.

_____ 5. Ex post facto research involves examining the aftereffects of the experimental manipulation employed by the researcher.

_____ 6. Null results generally only have one interaction.

_____ 7. An important criterion for a good dependent variable is reliability.

_____ 8. When the dependent variable is restricted to a narrow range near the top of the scale of measurement this indicates a ceiling effect.

_____ 9. Experimental control is usually better in three experiments each employing one independent variable than it is in a single experiment employing three independent variables.

_____10. An interaction is obtained when the effect produced by one independent variable is not the same at different levels of another independent variable.

_____11. Whenever interaction effects are obtained it does not make sense to consider separately the effects of each independent variable involved in the interaction.

ESSAY QUESTIONS

1. Define the three types of variables involved in an experiment, giving an example of each type of variable.

2. What are null results? What are the reasons why an otherwise valid experiment might produce null results?

3. What is an interaction? How do interactions affect the way in which the results of an experiment are interpreted?

CHAPTER 6.
Experimental Design

SUMMARY

In a well designed experiment we can make valid causal statements about the results and the experiment is said to be internally valid. There are a number of decisions that researchers must make when designing an experiment. First, the researcher must decide how to assign subjects to the various levels of the independent variable(s). In a between-subjects design each subject receives only one level of the independent variable, whereas in a within-subjects design each subject is given all levels of the independent variable. There are pros and cons to both types of designs and the researcher must carefully consider these issues when designing an experiment. If a between-subjects design is employed, then the researcher must try to ensure that the various groups of subjects are equivalent prior to the introduction of the independent variable. When a within-subject design is selected the researcher must try to minimize any carryover effects from the early treatments affecting behavior in a later portion of the experiment. It is also possible to treat some independent variables as between-subjects and others as within-subjects in the same experiment. Such designs are called mixed designs.

Finally, most experiments contain some control group (between-subjects design) or control condition (within-subjects design). These control conditions provide a baseline against which performance levels in other conditions may be compared.

KEY TERMS

balanced latin square

baseline

between-subjects design

carryover effects

control condition

counterbalancing

individual differences

internal validity

Latin-square design

matching

randomization

subject attrition

within-subjects design

PROGRAMMED REVIEW

1. A good experiment allows the researcher to state that changes in the independent variable _____ the observed changes in the dependent variable.

2. Experiments that lead to valid results are said to be _____ valid.

3. In the "executive monkey" experiments reported by Brady and his colleagues, the independent variable was (describe briefly)

   _____

   _____

4. Weiss (1971) showed that animals which respond at a _____ rate are likely to get ulcers, whether they are helpless or in control.

5. An experimental design in which each subject receives all levels of the independent variable is called a _____-subjects design.

6. The first design decision an experimenter must make is how to assign _____ to the various levels of the independent variable.

7. An experiment in which each subject is assigned to a particular level of the independent variable is called a _____-subjects design.

8. In any between-subjects experiment the researcher must strive to minimize differences among the _____ _____ that may exist before the experiment begins.

9. When the technique of matching is used to equate the various treatment groups the experimenter is trying to match on the basis of important _____ characteristics.

10. Matching is done on the basis of the most likely _____ variables.

11. When one or more of the subjects in an experiment do not complete the experiment this introduces the problem of subject _____.

12. The technique known as _____ is used to ensure the formation of equivalent groups of subject by giving each subject an equal opportunity to serve in any condition of the experiment.

13. Experimental design is concerned with the logic of _____ experiments.

14. The preferred technique for assigning subjects to experimental conditions is the _____ technique.

15. The _____-subjects design is generally the more efficient design.

16. If participation in one treatment condition is likely to affect performance in another treatment condition, then we would say that _____ effects pose a problem in this experiment.

17. The problem with using randomization to minimize carry-over effects is that a large number of _____ are required.

18. Complete _____ ensures that all possible treatment orders are used.

19. In a balanced _____-_____ design every experimental condition is preceded and followed equally often by every other condition.

20. If two Latin squares were needed to counterbalance the order of treatment presentations, than there must have been a(n) _____ number of treatment conditions.

21. A _____ design is one that employs both within- and between-subjects variable.

22. In its simplest form, a _____ group is the group that does not receive the levels of interest of the independent variable.

23. A control condition provides a _____ against which some other variable of the experiment may be compared.

24. Suppose your independent variable is likely to exert a permanent effect on your subjects. What type of design should you employ in this case?

_____

25. What type of design should be employed if there are large individual differences among the subjects in your sample?

_____

EXPERIMENTAL PROJECT

If a person is asked to solve several problems in succession, all of which are solvable by one procedure, the person will tend to continue using this procedure, even when a much simpler solution to the problem exists. Luchins (1942) performed a number of experiments in which he demonstrated this effect of Einstellung (mental set). In this experimental project you are going to replicate part of Luchins' original demonstration,

after which you will be given a chance to see if you can design
a better research project for examining the effect of mental set
on problem solving.

You will need at least two volunteers for this experiment,
although six or eight would probably be a more appropriate
sample size. Divide your subjects into two groups of equal
size. (Question: How are you going to assign subjects to
groups? Maybe you had better read the whole Experimental
Project and then decided how to assign subjects!) The subjects
will be told that their task is to obtain a specific volume of
water, using empty jars with varying capacities as their
measuring devices. There will be 8 problems in all, and these
are listed below.

Problem: Given these jars, obtain the following amounts:

Problem	Given Jars of these Capacities			Obtain
	A	B	C	
1	29	3	--	20
2	21	127	3	100
3	14	163	25	99
4	18	43	10	5
5	9	42	6	21
6	20	59	4	31
7	23	49	3	20
8	15	39	3	18

(These numbers represent the quart-capacity of the jars.)

All subjects are given the following information. The
subjects' task is to use the 3 jars available for that problem

obtain exactly the amount of water needed to solve the problem. There is an unlimited water supply.

Subjects in both the experimental group and control groups are first shown how to solve problem number 1: Fill the 29 quart jar, then use that jar to fill (and then empty) the 3 quart jar 3 times, thus leaving exactly 20 quarts of water in the larger jar.

Subjects in the experimental group then receive problems 2 through 8. The experimenter will demonstrate how to solve problem 2 (i.e., fill jar b, use this jar to fill jar once and jar c twice, thus leaving 100 quarts of water in jar b; 127 - 21 - 3 - 3 = 100). The experimental subjects are then allowed to solve problems 3 through 8.

The control group subjects move directly from problem 1 to problems 7 and 8.

Ask your subjects to describe the method they used to solve problems 7 and 8. On the basis of these descriptions you may classify how your subjects solved the problems, by the indirect route (i.e., 49 - 23 - 3 - 3 Problem 7) or the direct route (i.e., 23 - 3 Problem 7).

The dependent variable in this experiment might be the percentage of subjects who use a direct route for both problems 7 and 8. Which of your two groups showed a higher percentage of direct solutions? Do you think that the control group in this experiment was the appropriate one? Can you think of another possible control condition? (Hint: How many problems in all were given to each group.) Could the effect of mental set be studied using a within-subjects design? Can you think of another dependent variable that might be used in this experiment?

REFERENCE

Luchins, A.S. (1942). Mechanization in problem solving. Psychological Monographs. 54, No. 6 (Whole No. 248).

EXPERIMENTAL DILEMMA

A researcher is interested in studying the effect of environmental stress on the performance of various mental tasks. The environmental stressor is the temperature level in the experimental chamber. The researcher selects three different temperatures (40 F, 70 F, and 90 F) for the levels of stress to be included in the experiment. Since this is an experiment involving some risk to the subjects, the researcher employs male undergraduates to serve as subjects. The mental task selected for the first experiment is a choice reaction time task in which one of four stimulus lights comes on and the subject is to respond by pressing one of four buttons as quickly as possible. The researcher thinks that stressful environments will make subjects respond faster.

The researcher tests each subject in each condition during the 90 minute testing session. Each subject is first tested in the 70 condition, then the 90 condition, and finally in the 40 condition. Subjects receive 30 trials in each condition.

The results showed that the subjects mean reaction times for the three conditions were as follows:

Temperature	Mean Reaction Time
40 F	430 msec
70 F	525 msec
90 F	487 msec

Statistical analysis of the mean reaction times revealed that each of the three conditions was reliably different from the other two conditions. The researcher concluded that thermal stress improves reaction time. Do you agree with this conclusion?

MULTIPLE CHOICE QUESTIONS

_____ 1. In principle, experiments are designed to allow statements about

    a. causation.

    b. contiguity.

    c. correlation.

    d. relatedness.

    e. both c and d

_____ 2. The results of the early "executive-monkey" studies were invalid because

    a. the shocks used to induce stress were themselves capable of producing ulcers.

    b. the subjects assigned to the "executive" and "co-worker" conditions were different even prior to the beginning of the experiment.

    c. it is not valid to compare directly the results of animal research and human behavior.

    d. the differences between the experimental and control groups reflect correlations and not true causal relations.

_____ 3. In a simple between-subjects experimental design, each subject is given _____ level of the independent variable; in a within-subjects design each subject is given _____ level of the independent variable.

    a. one; one

    b. each; one

    c. one; each

    d. each; each

_____ 4. The purpose of good experimental design is to

    a. minimize extraneous or uncontrolled variation.

    b. come up with interesting research ideas.

    c. increase the likelihood that an experiment will produce internally valid results.

    d. avoid carry-over effects.

    e. both a and c

_____ 5. Which of the following is <u>not</u> a problem associated with between-subjects designs?

    a. the between-subjects design is a conservative design

    b. carry-over effect

    c. unequal treatment groups prior to the introduction of the independent variable

    d. subject attrition

_____ 6. The difference between a within-subjects design and a between-subjects design is that

    a. fewer subjects are needed in a between-subjects design.

    b. each subject serves as his or her own control in within-subject designs.

    c. confounding cannot occur with between-subjects designs.

    d. a given subject's behavior is measured only once in within-subjects designs.

_____ 7. A major disadvantage of between-subjects designs is that

    a. the effect of one treatment may alter the effectiveness of later treatments.

    b. subject differences may obscure treatment effects.

    c. one must use fewer independent variable.

    d. one can use only one dependent variable.

_____ 8. In order to obtain equivalent groups in between-subjects designs, you can

    a. randomly assign subjects to the various treatment groups.

    b. use each subject as his or her own control.

    c. attempt to match subjects on variables that are relevant.

    d. all of the above

    e. both a and c

_____ 9. One reason for preferring randomization to matching for establishing group equivalence is that

    a. we do not know all the relevant variables to match.

    b. randomization involves less confounding.

    c. counterbalancing does not require randomization.

    d. randomization guarantees group equivalence.

_____10. For between-subjects designs, randomization and matching are techniques used in an attempt to

a. prevent treatment carry-over effects.

b. ensure that the groups are equivalent at the start of the experiment.

c. minimize experimenter effects.

d. minimize demand characteristics.

e. both c and d

_____11. In within-subjects designs, counterbalancing is used to

a. enable the experimenter to evaluate possible treatment order effects.

b. assign subjects to treatment groups.

c. eliminate the effects of treatment order.

d. all of the above

_____12. In a completely counterbalanced experimental design

a. each group of subjects receives a different treatment.

b. every subject receives every treatment.

c. all possible treatment orders are used.

d. the treatment orders are randomized.

e. both b and c

_____13. In a balanced Latin square design

     a. each treatment appears once in each row.

     b. each treatment appears once in each column.

     c. each treatment precedes and follows every other treatment equally often.

     d. all of the above

     e. both a and b

_____14. A mixed design is one in which

     a. there is one independent and one dependent variable.

     b. at least one independent variable is tested within-subjects and the other independent variable(s) is (are) tested between-subjects.

     c. one independent variable is manipulated and the other independent variable(s) is (are) controlled.

     d. each subject receives a mixture of treatment conditions.

_____15. A control group or a control condition is included in an experiment to

     a. evaluate experimenter effects and demand effects.

     b. provide a baseline against which the variable of interest can be compared.

     c. prevent ceiling or floor effects.

     d. increase the generalizability of the results.

_____16. In an experiment designed to investigate the effects of alcohol on appetite, if drinks X and Y contain 0.5 and 1.0 ounces of vodka in orange juice, respectively, and drink Z contains only orange juice then the control group in the experiment should receive

a. drink X.

b. drink Y.

c. drink Z.

d. nothing to drink.

e. X, Y, and Z in a counterbalanced order.

TRUE - FALSE QUESTIONS

_____ 1. Experiments are internally valid in principle.

_____ 2. A major concern in experimental design is preventing carry-over effects in within-subjects designs.

_____ 3. The first design decision an experimenter must make is what levels of the independent variable should be used.

_____ 4. A within-subjects design is more conservative than a between-subjects design.

_____ 5. If an experimenter suspects that the effects of one treatment may linger on to alter behavior in a later condition, then she should use a counterbalanced within-subjects design.

_____ 6. The technique of counterbalancing is used in within-subjects designs to eliminate the effects of treatment order.

_____ 7. One difficulty with matching is that the experimenter cannot know all the potentially relevant dimensions on which to match subjects.

_____ 8. Subject attrition has a less detrimental effect when group characteristics are determined by an unbiased procedure, as compared to a matching procedure.

_____ 9. Random assignment of subjects to conditions guarantees that treatment groups will be equal prior to the administration of the independent variable.

_____10. Within-subjects designs are generally more efficient than between-subjects designs.

_____11. Carry-over effects are eliminated in a completely counterbalanced design.

_____12. Unless the number of experimental conditions is greater than 7, a single balanced Latin square is sufficient for counterbalancing treatment orders within an experiment.

_____13. Counterbalancing can be used for assigning treatment orders as well as determining the order of testing when more than one independent variable is used.

_____14. The control group is the group that does not receive the levels of interest of the independent variable.

_____15. Most subject variables require the use of a between-subject design.

ESSAY QUESTIONS

1. Briefly describe the design flaw in the original "executive monkey" studies. How could these experiments have been redesigned in order to avoid the design flaw?

2. Discuss the advantages and disadvantages of between-subjects and within-subjects designs.

3. Describe what is meant by subject attrition. How can subject attrition affect the results of an experiment? What types of experimental designs would you expect to be least affected by subject attrition?

CHAPTER 7.
Complex Experimentation

SUMMARY

Multifactor experiments employ more than one independent
variable and any or all of these variables may have more than
two levels. In multifactor experiments, the independent
variables may be manipulated entirely between-subjects, entirely
within-subjects, or some of the factors may be manipulated
within-subjects and the remaining factors manipulated between-
subjects (mixed design). When all levels of each independent
variable are employed in an experiment this represents a
factorial design in which all possible combinations of all
levels of the independent variable are examined. In a between-
subjects factorial design the number of independent groups is a
multiplicative function of the number of levels of each of the
independent variables (e.g., in a 2 x 2 x 4 design there are 16
independent groups).

Multifactor experiments allow the researcher to identify both
main effects of independent variables and interactions among
independent variables. Interaction effects can only be observed
when there are two or more independent variables manipulated
within the same experiment. When more than two independent
variables are included within an experiment there may be higher-

order interactions involving each of the independent variables. Such higher-order interactions may be difficult to interpret.

Control procedures in multifactor experiments are needed to guard against many different types of confounding. While these control procedures can often be quite complicated, they are in principle quite similar to those control procedures used in single factor experiments.

KEY TERMS

block randomization

crossover interaction

discounting cue

interaction

main effects

matched-group design

mixed designs

random-groups designs

repeated-measures designs

sleeper effect

treatments x treatments x subjects design

2 x 2 factorial design

PROGRAMMED REVIEW

1. Multifactor experiments are likely to have better _____ validity than single-factor experiments.

2. Complex multifactor experiments allow the researcher to make complex causal statements which should increase _____ validity.

3. The phenomenon of an increase in the effectiveness of a persuasive message is called the _____ effect.

4. To obtain a sleeper effect, the persuasive message must be accompanied by a _____ _____.

5. In a 2 x 2 factorial design there are two _____ variables, each with two _____.

6. A factorial experiment includes all possible combinations of all levels of the _____ _____.

7. The effect of a single independent variable is called a _____ effect.

8. An _____ effect occurs when the effects of one independent variable depend upon the level of another independent variable.

9. In an ideal experiment subjects would be randomly _____ and then randomly _____ to treatment conditions.

10. In a between-subjects design we want to make sure that the characteristics of the _____ are not confounded with group membership.

11. Two techniques for achieving unbiased assignment of subjects to conditions are to _____ assign subjects to treatment conditions or to use a balanced _____ _____ to determine group membership.

12. In general researchers try to avoid experimental designs in which potential _____ variables can interact with the independent variable(s).

13. A design in which the assignment of subjects to conditions is unbiased is called a _____ - _____ design.

14. In a matched-groups design the _____ are matched on potentially important variable.

15. A _____-subjects design automatically controls for individual differences.

16. A _____-subjects design requires fewer subjects than does a comparable _____-subjects design.

17. The reduced number of subjects tested in a within-subjects design may require that the experimenter increase the number of observations per _____.

18. When there are two independent variables there are _____ possible main effect(s) and _____ possible interaction(s).

19. Whenever an independent variable is manipulated within-subjects there is a possibility of potential _____ effects.

20. Carryover effects can be guarded against by _____ or a _____ randomization in which the order of treatments would be randomized two or more times.

21. In a _____ randomized design every condition is tested before a particular condition is tested again.

22. _____ designs have one or more between-subjects independent variables and one or more within-subjects variable.

23. In a mixed design, the independent variable with strong carryover effects is typically manipulated as a _____ - subjects variable.

24. Another name for a within-subjects design in which there are a large number of practice trials is a _____ _____ design.

25. Weinstock (1958) employed a mixed design to study the effects of reinforcement history on performance levels: _____ was the within-subjects variable and _____ of _____ was the between-subjects variable.

26. In Weinstock's (1958) experiment, the trials in which no reinforcement was given are called _____ trials.

EXPERIMENTAL PROJECT

Some memory researchers have found that information is better remembered when the presentations of study material are spaced apart from one another than when the presentations are massed together. That is, you will probably do better on an exam if you study the test material periodically throughout the course than if you just cram the night before the test. As an illustration of this general principle, conduct a study in which you manipulate spaced versus massed presentation as one of your independent variables. In order to better understand the concept of multi-factor designs, add another manipulation of type of study material, namely whether study words occur with high or low frequency in natural language. (Lists of high and low frequency words may be obtained from the Kucera and Francis word norms found in <u>Computational analysis of present-day American English</u>. Providence, RI: Brown University Press, 1967.) Manipulate spaced versus massed presentation between subjects and test word frequency as a within-subjects factor.

The study material for all subjects will consist of a 100 word list - half of the words should be high frequency items and half should be low frequency items. Test the same number of subjects in the spaced and massed groups and equate total study time across the two groups. Subjects in the spaced group should be given the time lapse between presentations, which should be the same for all subjects in the group. Give a 10 minute free recall test immediately following the third presentation. Give the massed group the stimulus list and have them study it for 30 minutes. Following study test them in exactly the same manner as the spaced group.

Score the data for a general measure of number of words recalled for the spaced versus massed conditions and for number of high frequency words versus number of low frequency words recalled across groups. These measure will allow you to assess main effects. You will also need a breakdown of the number of high and low frequency words recalled in each study group in order to look at interaction effects. Plot the number of words recalled as a function of word frequency and study condition. Do you find any main effects? Is there any evidence of an interaction? Did it appear that ceiling effects or floor effects might be present in your experiment? What do these results suggest to you concerning your present study strategies?

EXPERIMENTAL DILEMMAS

1. An experimenter examined the effects of test expectancy (i.e., expecting a recall test of a recognition test) on performance of different types of tests as a function of the

to their imageability. That is, high imagery words were those for which subjects could readily form a mental image (e.g., apple) and low imagery words were items for which mental images could not be easily formed (e.g., decision). All of those variables were manipulated between-subjects. Thus the design was a 2 (test expectancy: recall versus recognition) x 2 (test type: recall versus recognition) x 2 (imagery: high versus low) multifactor design. Subjects were given a 25 item word list to study overnight and were told that they would be given either a recall or recognition test the next day. Half of the subjects were told to expect a recall test and half were told to expect recognition. In addition, half of the subjects were given a list of low imagery words and half studied high imagery words. Subjects were tested upon returning to the laboratory. Half of the subjects received the type of test that they expected and half were given the unexpected test type. The following results were obtained. The numbers represent percent correct on the memory tests.

	LOW IMAGERY		HIGH IMAGERY	
	TEST GIVEN		TEST GIVEN	
TEST EXPECTED	RECALL	RECOGNITION	RECALL	RECOGNITION
RECALL	70	75	99	99
RECOGNITION	40	85	92	98

There were main effects of test type, test expectancy, and imagery. There was a test type x test expectancy interaction and there was a three way interaction of test type, test expectancy, and imagery. The experimenter concluded that performance on recognition tests was superior to performance on recall tests and that subjects performed better in general when led to expect recall than when expecting recognition. She also argued that high imagery words were better remembered than low imagery words. Furthermore, performance was enhanced when the type of test given matched the type of test expected. With regard to the three way interaction, the experimenter concluded that when subjects study low imagery words recognition performance is superior to recall when subjects expect recall but that there is no such difference when high imagery words are studied.

Is there anything wrong with the design or procedures used in this experiment? Do you agree with the conclusion? How might you design an experiment to test the hypotheses under consideration.

2. A researcher hypothesizes that subjects will be able to recall words better when given instructions to form images of the words during presentation than if given no special instructions. In addition the experimenter wishes to examine the effects of delaying the recall test for different periods of time. It is expected that recall performance will drop with increased delay but it is not known how this variable might interact with the encoding manipulation. Two groups of subjects are tested: The imagery group is instructed to form mental images of each word as it is presented, but the No Imagery group is given no explicit instructions. All subjects are presented with the same list of 50 concrete nouns at the rate of 10 seconds each. Each of the two groups is divided so that half of the subjects are given a free recall test one week later. All subjects are allowed 5 minutes for the recall test. The results obtained are presented below.

DELAY	INSTRUCTIONS	
	IMAGERY	NO IMAGERY
1 HOUR	75%	50%
1 WEEK	50%	25%

There was a main effect of instruction condition and of delay condition but there was no instruction x delay interaction. From these data the experimenter concluded that memory performance is enhanced when subjects are instructed to form mental images of input items and that performance decreases as the delay between input and test increases, but that the delay manipulation does not differentially affect performance as a function of input condition. Do you agree with these conclusions? If not, why?

MULTIPLE CHOICE QUESTIONS

_____ 1. Which of the following is not a reason for doing multi-factor experiments instead of several single-factor experiments?

    a. increase the internal validity of the experiments

    b. increase the generality of the results

    c. fewer observations per subject are required in a multi-factor experiment

    d. multi-factor experiments attempt to match the complexity of forces that combine to influence our thought and behavior

    e. all of the above

_____ 2. A factorial experiment
  a. is a between-subjects design.
  b. involves testing all possible combinations of all
     levels of each independent variable.
  c. allows the researcher to observe interaction
     effects.
  d. all of the above
  e. both b and c

_____ 3. In a 3 x 3 factorial experiment, how many effects can
     we determine?
  a. 2
  b. 3
  c. 4
  d. 6
  e. 9

_____ 4. In a 3 x 2 between-subjects design, there are
     _____ independent groups and each subject serves
     in _____ conditions in the experiment.
  a. 5; 1
  b. 5; 2
  c. 6; 1
  d. 6; 2
  e. 6; 6

_____ 5. According to the dissociation hypothesis explanation of
     the sleeper effect,
  a. there is less opinion change over time.
  b. the link between the message and discounting cue
     strengthens over time.
  c. the message is remembered while the discounting cue
     is forgotten.
  d. the discounting cue is easier to retrieve.

_____ 6. What does it mean when we say that a main effect was obtained in a between-subjects factorial experiment?

    a. The scores obtained under one level of an independent variable were different than the scores obtained under another level of that independent variable.

    b. The mean score from one level of an independent variable was different from the mean score of one level of a different independent variable.

    c. Overall, one independent variable had a larger effect on the dependent variable than did the other independent variables.

    d. The effect of the independent variable was different for different dependent variables.

_____ 7. Which of the following describes an interaction effect?

    a. The scores obtained at one level of the independent variable were different than the scores obtained at another level of the independent variable.

    b. The observed effect of one independent variable depends on the level of other independent variables.

    c. The effect of one independent variable was larger for one dependent variable than for another.

    d. The nature of an interaction can only be described when the type of experimental design is known.

_____ 8. In a factorial experiment, the number of factors is the number of _____ variables and the number of levels is the number of instances of each _____ variable tested in the experiment.

    a. dependent; dependent

    b. independent; independent

    c. dependent; independent

    d. independent; dependent

_____ 9. An interaction effect occurs when

      a. performance in one condition is superior to that in another condition.

      b. performance changes across levels of the independent variable.

      c. the effect of the dependent variable reflects performance in more than one experimental condition.

      d. the effects of one independent variable change depending on the level of another independent variable

_____10. An experiment with two factors and two levels of each factor with all possible combinations of these factors is called a _____ factorial.

      a. 2 x 2

      b. 2 x 2 x 2

      c. 2

      d. 2 x 4 x 8

_____ 11. Complex multifactor experiments

      a. can be efficient.

      b. can produce results that are difficult to interpret.

      c. allow us to observe both main effects and interaction effects.

      d. all of the above

_____12. An experiment in which the effects of more than one independent variable are examined simultaneously is called a _____ experiment.

      a. mixed factor

      b. multifactor

      c. single factor

      d. within-subjects

_____13. An experimenter studied the effects of education level on soft drink preference. Both Ph.D.'s and high school graduates preferred Coke to Pepsi but the effect was much larger for high school graduates than for Ph.D.'s. The results indicate

a. a main effect and an interaction.

b. a main effect with no interaction.

c. an interaction with no main effect.

d. neither a main effect nor an interaction.

_____14. When experimental results are presented in a figure, the presence of an interaction is indicated by:

a. positive or negative slope of the lines.

b. one line that is higher than another.

c. two (or more) lines that are not parallel to the x-axis.

d. two (or more) lines that are not parallel by the y-axis.

e. lines that are not parallel with one another.

_____15. In a between-subjects factorial design the researcher must make an effort to:

a. ensure that the characteristics of the subject are not confounded with group membership.

b. equate treatment conditions across the independent groups.

c. administer all levels of the independent variable to each subject.

d. control for carry-over effects.

_____16. The within-subjects design is often used instead of a between-subjects design because

a. of carry-over effects.

b. the within-subjects design requires fewer subjects.

c. the within-subjects design control for individual differences.

d. there is not a problem in determining which subjects receive the identical treatment orders.

e. both b and c

_____17. Compared to a between-subjects random group factorial design, a within-subjects factorial design

a. requires matching subjects on relevant variables.

b. requires fewer subjects.

c. requires more observations per subject.

d. all of the above

e. both b and c

_____18. Under which of the following conditions would you want to avoid using a treatment x treatment x subjects design?

a. there are large individual subject differences

b. there are only a small number of subjects available for participation in the experiment

c. participation in one treatment condition may affect performance levels in another condition

d. many observations can be obtained from a single subject

e. all of the above

_____19. A mixed-design experiment is one that contains

a. an independent variable and a subject variable.

b. repeated measures and within-subjects factors.

c. two independent variables that produced an interaction.

d. at least one between-subject independent variable and one dependent variable.

_____20. The results of the Dewing and Hetherington (1974) study suggest that

a. imagery value of the solution word affects anagram solution time.

b. the type of hint given may influence anagram solution time.

c. for high imagery words a semantic clue aids anagram solution more than a structural clue.

d. for low imagery words a structural clue aids anagram solution more than a semantic clue.

e. all of the above

_____21. If a 6 x 6 balanced Latin square were used to determine the order of presentation of 6 treatment conditions, in what multiples would the experimenter have to test subjects in?

a. 6

b. 12

c. 18

d. 36

e. 216

_____22. The partial reinforcement effect is a phenomenon in which partial reinforcement schedules produce learning that

a. extinguishes more rapidly than learning on a continuous reinforcement schedule.

b. extinguishes at the same rate as does learning on a continuous reinforcement schedule.

c. does not extinguish as rapidly as does learning on a continuous reinforcement schedule.

d. the question cannot be answered since the rate of extinction depends upon whether the experiment used a within-subjects or a between-subject design.

TRUE-FALSE QUESTIONS

_____ 1. Multifactor experiments are more likely to have ecological validity than single-factor experiments.

_____ 2. If possible researchers should start off research in a new area by employing multifactor experiments since these designs are more efficient than single-factor experiments.

_____ 3. In a within-subjects design the number of groups of subjects is equal to the product of number of levels of the independent variable times the number of independent variable.

_____ 4. In a main effect one dependent variable shows a different pattern of results than the other dependent variable.

_____ 5. In order to obtain an interaction at least one of the factors involved in the interaction must have produced a significant main effect.

_____ 6. Main effects are more revealing than interaction effects.

_____ 7. In a random groups design the experimenter attempts to reduce random variability by equating subjects on variable other than the independent variable(s).

_____ 8. Within-subjects designs typically require few observations per subject because each subject serves as their own control.

_____ 9. The primary dangers inherent in treatment x treatment x subjects design are carryover effects.

_____10. Across test trials, block randomization would be less likely than complete randomization to confound test order and condition.

_____11. In a within-subjects design, the advantage of using a balanced Latin square to assign treatment orders (as opposed to randomization procedures) is that with the Latin square method each treatment would precede and follow every other treatment equally often.

ESSAY QUESTIONS

1. Briefly discuss the advantages and disadvantages of using multifactor experimental designs.

2. Describe several conditions under which it would be preferable to use a between-subjects design. When would a within-subjects design be preferable?

3. Consider an experimental design similar to the one in the chapter in which the discounting cue and delay of rating are manipulated in a factorial design. Make up patterns of results (different from those reported in the text) to sketch the following:

   a. Main effects of both variables with no interaction.

   b. An interaction effect but no main effects.

   c. Only one main effect and a significant interaction.

CHAPTER 8.
Small-N Experimentation

SUMMARY

In contrast to most control-group and control-condition designs, small-n research involves numerous observations on a small number of subjects. Psychophysics, operant conditioning, and clinical research represent three substantive areas in which small-n designs are typically used. In psychophysics small-n designs are used because they represent an economical approach for collecting data concerning the nature of the relation between psychological judgements and the physical properties of stimuli. In operant conditioning research small-n designs are used because these designs allow the researcher to make detailed observations under conditions that allow precise control of the experimental setting. In clinical research, the small-n design known as the case study is often used to make useful observations of unusual and special people.

Unlike classical psychophysics, signal detection theory suggests that there is no such thing as a sensory threshold. Signal detection theory postulates that perceptual responses are determined by both internal sensory processes and by the decision process, both of which may affect what is termed "the threshold" in classical psychophysics. Signal detection theory replaces the concept of a threshold with beta (a criterion in the decision-making process) and $\underline{d}'$ (a measure of stimulus strength).

In operant conditioning research a small number of organisms are studied intensively. A typical design that is used is the reversal design, or the ABA design, where A and B refer to different phases of the experiment. The A phases are often called baseline phases, and during these periods the subject behavior is observed without the introduction of the experimental treatment, which is introduced only during the B phase. One limitation of the reversal design is that oftentimes behavior levels do not return to baseline after the introduction of the treatment (i.e., there are carryover effects). Under these circumstances a multiple baseline design may be appropriate. Alternatively, the researcher may want to include more than one experimental treatment in order to determine which of these treatments actually controls behavior.

The chapter concludes with an example of small-$\underline{n}$ research of the study of memory in a patient with multiple personality disorder, in which a variety of memory tests, usually used in the context of full-scale experiments, were used in conjunction with a case study.

KEY TERMS

beta	noise
case study	receiver-operating-characteristic
criterion	(ROC)
$\underline{d}'$	reversal design (ABA)
decision process	sensory impression
false alarm	small-$\underline{n}$ designs
hit	theory of signal detection
internal distribution	

PROGRAMMED REVIEW

1. The _n_ in a small-_n_ design refers to the number of
    _____.

2. According to signal detection theory there is no such
    thing as a fixed _____.

3. Signal detection theory argues that both internal
    _____ and internal _____ processes are involved
    in perception.

4. Decisions depend upon the _____ and the _____
    associated with those decisions.

5. According to signal detection theory _____ is always
    present inside the human.

6. A stimulus, according to signal detection theory, produces
    an internal _____ of _____ impressions.

7. The hypothetical distributions called the _____
    distribution and _____ + _____ distribution both
    play a role in our perception.

8. In an signal detection experiment the observer must set a
    _____ to determine if a response will be Yes or No.
    This _____ is set by _____ process.

9. Identify the following types of trials.

Signal	Response	Trial is a
Present	Yes	(a)_____
Not Present	Yes	(b)_____

10. When we plot hits as a function of false alarms, as the
    decision criterion moves from conservative to liberal we
    obtain a curve known as the _____ - _____ -
    characteristic.

11. _d'_ refers to the _____ of the observer as is defined
    as the _____ _____ the signal and noise
    distributions.

12. The criteria of the decision process is called _____, and it refers to the _____ of the ROC function at the point of interest.

13. In Clark and Yang's (1974) experiment they found that acupuncture had an effect upon _____, but had no effect upon _____.

14. In an AB design, A represents the _____ condition and B represents the condition after the _____ variable had been introduced.

15. In the AB design the researcher cannot conclusively establish that the variable introduced during the B phase caused the change in behavior, because there is a _____ confounding inherent in this design.

16. Another name for the ABA design is the _____ design.

17. In the ABA design during the second A phase the _____ variable is no longer applied, but the _____ _____ is still recorded.

18. If the behavior during the second A phase of an ABA design, returns to the level of the first A phase, then we can conclude that the _____ variable applied during the _____ phase actually effected the change.

19. In the study by Hart et al. during the B phase the teacher attempted to _____ the crying behavior by not paying attention, while _____ Bill whenever he behaved in an appropriate manner.

20. In the Hart et al, study, the number of crying episodes _____ during the second _____ phase and _____ during both _____ phases.

21. Small-n designs often include _____ - _____ effects that prohibit the reversal design.

22. In Rose's (1978) experiment on the effects of artificial food colors on hyperactivity, the B and C phases include different _____ variables but the same _____ variable is employed in both phases.

23. Because Nissen's (1988) study of memory dysfunction in a patient with multiple personality disorder is based on a single subject, it is an example of a _____ _____.

24. Nissen found that faces shown to one personality (would be, would not be) _____ recognized by another personality.

25. Nissen found that words judged as to their pleasantness by one personality, (would be, would not be) _____ used in a word completion task by another personality, at a greater than chance rate.

EXPERIMENTAL PROJECT

The principles of operant conditioning are operating in many ways in our everyday lives. For example, pet owners often apply the principles of operant conditioning when attempting to train their pets. In this project you will have an opportunity to try and apply the principles of operant conditioning to conditioning another human's behavior. This project is essentially a partial replication of an earlier study reported by Verplanck (1955).

If attention from another person is reinforcing, then it should be possible to use attention as a reinforcer for increasing the frequency of some response. In this demonstration project a "point" system will be used to reinforce another person's behavior. The goal of this conditioning exercise is to increase the frequency with which a person makes opinionated statements.

The experiment requires one person to serve as a volunteer subject. The only materials needed are two sheets of paper, two pencils, and a timing device suitable for timing one minute intervals.

The experiment should be carried out in a quiet room in which the experiment can proceed uninterrupted for one hour. Once the experimenter and the subject are seated, the experimenter should read the following instructions:

In a moment I want you to begin talking. You are free to talk on whatever topic you wish. I will not be saying anything during the experiment, but do not let this silence bother you. Your task in the experiment is to work for points. You will receive a point each time I tap my pencil. As soon as you receive a point, record it on your score sheet by making a tally mark. Do you have any questions? (Answer any questions the subject may have).

If you have no (further) questions, please commence talking. Each time your subject makes an opinionated statement, tap your pencil to give your subject a point. You will have to decide what constitutes an opinionated statement, but reinforce such statements as "I believe that ...," "I feel that ...," "I think that ...," etc.

The experiment will consist of an acquisition phase and an extinction phase. During each of these phases the experimenter will keep track of the number of opinionated statements made by the subject. During the first 18 minutes, the experimenter should tap his pencil every time an opinionated statement is made. After the first 18 minutes these experimenter should stop "giving points" for opinionated statements, and should simply keep track of how many opinionated statements are made by the subject. Continue this extinction phase for 18 minutes. Finally, the record of the opinionated statements should reflect how many statements were made during minutes 1-3, 4-6, 7-10, etc.

After the experiment is completed, ask your subject if (s)he was aware of what (s)he was doing to receive points. Was your subject aware or unaware?

Was operant conditioning demonstrated? Was there a difference in the number of opinionated statements made during acquisition and extinction? Could operant conditioning could be applied to other aspects of human behavior?

REFERENCE

Verplanck, W.S. (1955). The operant, from rat to man: An introduction to some recent experiments on human behavior. Transcripts of the New York Academy of Science. 17. 594-601.

EXPERIMENTAL DILEMMAS

1. As part of an investigation of the effects of biorhythms on various physical and psychological abilities a researcher decided to measure absolute threshold early in the morning and then again late at night. Each morning the researcher went to his laboratory at 6:00 a.m. and tested his subjects' absolute threshold, using the method of limits to determine the absolute threshold for detecting a 400 hz tone embedded in white noise. At night the subjects reported to the University Sleep Lab to be tested. The Sleep Lab was equipped with a microcomputer which make it easy to test the subjects absolute threshold using the staircase method. As in the morning session, the subject's task was to detect the presence of a 400 hz tone embedded in white noise.

The results showed that, on average, the subjects' absolute threshold was lower in the morning than in the evening. That is, the absolute threshold stimulus intensity was lower in the morning than in the evening. The researcher concluded that time of day has an affect upon auditory absolute threshold, with people being more sensitive in the morning than in the afternoon.

Do you agree or disagree with this conclusion? Why or why not?

2. A psychologist interested in the effect of personality traits upon various psychological abilities decided to test whether introverts or extroverts are more sensitive to external stimulation. His hypothesis was that introverts, who are basically quiet, shy people, would be more sensitive to the external world than would extroverts, who he thought would be

more sensitive to internal stimulation. To test this hypothesis he decided to see which group of subjects would be better able to detect a very faint amount of pressure applied to the back of the hand.

Ten introverts and 10 extroverts were selected on the basis of a personality test. All subjects were paid for their participation. Subjects were each tested individually by the same experimenter. Subjects were blindfolded and then given 200 trials. On half of the trials, a very faint amount of pressure was applied to the back of the subjects hand by means of a mechanical device. The amount of pressure was constant for all subjects. On the remaining trials no pressure was applied to the subjects hand. All subjects were right handed, and only the right hand was used in the experiment. Finally, a different random order of pressure trials and no pressure trials was used for each subject. Subjects were not told how many trials there would be, only that there would be "a lot." No subject was told what percentage of trials would be "touch" trials.

Results showed that, averaged across subject, the extroverts responded correctly on 85% of the touch trials and were incorrect on 15% of these trials. Introverts, however were only correct on 70% of the touch trials, making 30% errors on these trials. These differences between groups were reliable.

The research concluded that these results indicated that extroverts were more sensitive than introverts, since they were correct on more of the touch trials (85% versus 70%). Since this was exactly the opposite of what he had predicted he decided that his hypothesis needed to be revised.

Do you agree with this conclusion? Why or why not? How would you design an experiment to test this hypothesis?

MULTIPLE CHOICE QUESTIONS

_____ 1. The 'n' in small-n designs refers to the number of

    a. dependent variables.

    b. independent variables.

    c. measurements.

    d. subjects.

_____ 2. In small-n designs, usually _____ observations are made of _____ subjects.

    a. few; few

    b. few; many

    c. many; few

    d. many; many

_____ 3. According to signal detection theory perceptual responses are controlled by _____ and _____ processes.

    a. sensory impressions; criterion

    b. thresholds; criterion

    c. sensory impressions; decision

    d. sensory impressions; bias

    e. neural events; criterion

_____ 4. In signal detection theory, moving the criteria to the left will

    a. increase the hit rate.

    b. increase the false alarm rate.

    c. decrease d'.

    d. all of the above

    e. a and c

_____ 5. You must decide whether or not to accept a blind date. By accepting the date you risk spending a boring evening. On the other hand, you also stand a chance of meeting a fascinating person and possibly beginning a beautiful relationship. According to signal detection theory, for your decision you would adopt:
   a. a conservative criterion.
   b. a liberal criterion.
   c. an ultraconservative criterion.
   d. none of the above.

_____ 6. According to signal detection theory, detecting a signal when both signal and noise are present is a:
   a. hit.
   b. miss.
   c. false alarm.
   d. correct rejection.

_____ 7. According to signal detection theory, detecting a signal when only noise is present is called a:
   a. hit.
   b. miss.
   c. false alarm.
   d. correct rejection.

_____ 8. In signal detection theory, the value of $\underline{d}'$ is the:
   a. mean of the noise distribution.
   b. mean of the signal distribution.
   c. distance between the means of the signal and noise distributions.
   d. point at which the criterion divides the noise and signal distributions.

_____ 9. In a Receiver Operating Characteristic (ROC) function:

    a. d' is plotted as a function of the criterion (beta).

    b. hits are plotted as a function of false alarm.

    c. hits are plotted as a function of d'.

    d. false alarms are plotted as a function of the criterion (beta).

_____ 10. In signal detection theory, the position of the criterion is determined by:

    a. the decision process.

    b. the sensory process.

    c. the stimulus intensity.

    d. the mean of the signal distribution.

_____ 11. In an ABA design, A refers to _____ and B refers to _____ .

    a. baseline; experimental treatment

    b. baseline; dependent variable

    c. experimental treatment; baseline

    d. experimental treatment; dependent variable

_____ 12. When using an AB design in the clinical treatment of maladaptive behavior, the first step is to:

    a. extinguish the maladaptive behavior.

    b. reinforce adaptive behaviors.

    c. obtain a baseline of the maladaptive behavior.

    d. both a and b

_____ 13. An AB design is a poor design because

    a. there may be a confounding of uncontrolled factors and level of the independent variable.

    b. it is only appropriate to use with a small-n design.

    c. experimenter bias usually plays a role.

    d. it is impossible to obtain a stable baseline measure with only a single baseline phase.

    e. both b and c

_____14. The ABA design
   a. is a small-_n_ design.
   b. is a between-subjects design.
   c. is also called a reversal design.
   d. all of the above
   e. both a and c

_____15. Which of the following is considered the more optimum small-_n_ design?
   a. AB designs
   b. ABA designs
   c. ABC designs
   d. ABB designs

_____16. Rose's study of the effects of oatmeal cookies and artificial food coloring on hyperactivity showed that hyperactivity was highest
   a. with the K-P diet used in the A phase.
   b. with oatmeal cookies, both colored and uncolored.
   c. with artificially colored oatmeal cookies.
   d. with artificially colored K-P diet.

_____17. Nissen, et al. (1988) showed that a patient with a multiple personality disorder could
   a. easily remember things shown to any of her other personalities.
   b. could only remember things shown to the same personality that was being tested.
   c. had better than chance recognition memory for faces shown to another personality.
   d. had a better than chance probability of using a word shown to another personality in a word completion task.

_____18. Nissen's study of memory dysfunction in multiple personality disorders was an example of
a. an ABA design.
b. a case study.
c. operant-conditioning.
d. signal detection research.

TRUE - FALSE QUESTIONS

_____ 1. Typically in small-n research, many observations are made on a small number of subjects.

_____ 2. Small-n research is used when Mill's joint method of agreement and difference is not appropriate.

_____ 3. According to signal detection theory, whether an observer responds Yes or No depends upon the sensory impression and the decision criterion.

_____ 4. Signal detection theory defines threshold in terms of the observer's decision criterion.

_____ 5. In signal detection theory, the distance between the means of the signal and noise distributions is called d'.

_____ 6. According to signal detection theory, moving the criterion to the left will increase the number of false alarms and the number of hits.

_____ 7. The AB design is a very poor small-n design because the researcher cannot be sure the obtained effect is due to the independent variable.

_____ 8. The advantage of the ABA design over the AB design is that in the ABA design the second A phase allows the researcher to determine whether the behavior will return to baseline levels when the experimental treatment is no longer applied.

_____ 9. In a patient with a multiple personality disorder, the more ambiguous the memory task, the more likely it is that one personality will have access to information presented to another personality.

ESSAY QUESTIONS

1. Hypnosis has sometimes been used to improve a person's memory for an event that the person witnessed. Research has suggested that the effect of hypnosis is on the criterion for recall, rather than increasing $\underline{d}'$ for past events. How can this be understood? Suggest a study to investigate this possibility.

2. Describe briefly the key concepts underlying signal detection theory. How does signal detection theory approach the notion of a threshold?

3. Why is an ABA design preferable to an AB design? What conclusions can you draw from an ABA design that you cannot draw from an AB design?

CHAPTER 9.
Quasi-Experimentation

SUMMARY

In quasi-experimental research there is no direct control over the independent variables. As a result, quasi-experiments do not allow us to make statements about causal relations. In quasi-experiments either the effects of natural "treatments" are observed or specific subject variables are considered.

One-shot case studies and interrupted-time-series designs represent two quasi-experimental designs that exhibit low internal validity. The deviant-case analysis represents an attempt to obtain a "control" group in case-study research. Interrupted-time-series designs have been used effectively in applied research. Since the experimenter often does not control the assignment of subjects to groups of the manipulation of variables in ex post facto designs, there are often problems of confounding. However, there are statistical techniques available that allow for control in these situations, one of which is the cross-lagged correlation procedure. One way in which possible confounding of subjects variables may be avoided is by matching experimental and control subjects on some other relevant dimensions. This matching technique is not foolproof, however, in that it may lead to regression artifacts.

In developmental studies, including studies on intelligence, age is often a subject variable of interest. There are several ways in which the effects of age be examined. Cross-sectional designs involve testing subjects of different age groups and comparing performance across these groups. A major problem with this approach is that other factors are often confounded with age, thus preventing any causal inferences. The confoundings inherent in cross-sectional designs are eliminated in longitudinal designs where the same subjects are repeatedly tested over a period of several years. Results of longitudinal designs may be contaminated, however, by the influence of historical events occurring during the course of the study. These difficulties may be remedied through the use of cross-sequential designs in which subjects born in successive years are tested in later successive years. Since cross-sequential designs embed cross-sectional and longitudinal designs within them, they permit less ambiguous interpretations of the effects of age as a subject variable.

KEY TERMS

cross-sectional method

cross-sequential design

history

interaction

interrupted-time-series design

longitudinal method

matching

maturation

mortality

nonequivalent control group

observation-treatment-observation

one-shot case study

quasi-experiment

regression artifact

regression to the mean

selection bias

subject variable

synergism

time lag design

PROGRAMMED REVIEW

1. Quasi-experiments allow the researcher to examine variables that would be _____ to manipulate directly.

2. Most quasi-experiments involving naturally occurring events are similar in structure to small-n _____ designs.

3. Quasi-experiments of the general form observation-treatment-observation are not true reversal designs because

    (a)_____

    _____

    and

    (b)_____

    _____

4. Two threats to internal validity with naturally occurring treatments are the _____ of the subject and any changes in the _____ that occur over time.

5. In a nonequivalent control group design the experimenter attempts to _____ two groups after one group has received some treatments.

6. The primary threat to internal validity associated with the one-shot case study is the lack of a _____ _____.

7. In a typical case study the researcher gains control by increasing the _____ of observations.

8. In long-term time series studies the participants may be unavailable late in the study, a confounding factor that is called _____. This confounding would lead to a special form of _____ bias.

9. The difficulties of the interrupted-time-series design are magnified when the _____ of the treatment is delayed or masked by other variables.

10. Sex, height, and I.Q. are all _____ variables.

11. Designs employing subject variables essentially produce _____ between variables.

12. A problem inherent in studies employing subject variables is that whatever results are obtained may be caused by _____ variables.

13. One way to avoid confounding with subject variables is _____.

14. Matching often greatly reduces _____ size.

15. Synergism of two variables means that the two variables do not have _____ effects but rather they _____.

16. Matching may lead to _____ artifacts.

17. In a _____ design the same subject is tested repeatedly over a long time period.

18. In a _____-_____ design the researcher selects children from different ages and observes their behavior on one occasion.

19. Age is not a true _____ variable.

20. As an individual goes through life he maintains the same _____, or group of people born at approximately the same time period.

21. A time-lag design attempts to determine the effects of the time of _____ while holding _____ constant.

EXPERIMENTAL PROJECT

One "naturally occurring" event for college and university students is examinations. Hence these events represent an excellent opportunity to use a quasi-experimental approach to test a hypotheses. From studies of the effect of various schedules of reinforcement on behavior patterns, we know that there is often a post-response pause that follows reinforcement when the organism is on a partial reinforcement schedule. It has been suggested that a similar 'pause' occurs following major examinations. (Perhaps you have experienced this firsthand.)

To study this phenomenon, you will need to select one or two persons who will agree to allow you to monitor their study behavior. If you use a single subject, then record (or ask the person to record) the number of hours spent studying over a two-week period that contains an examination approximately mid-way through the observation period. If you use two persons, then for the second person record study behaviors during a two-week period in which no-examinations occur.

Before you rush out and carry out this project there are several things you will need to consider. Is the fact that you are monitoring the person's behavior likely to change the person's behavior? If you use two persons, how are you going to match these individuals? What possible threats to internal validity are inherent in this design? External validity?

Once you collect the data, are you tempted to say that having the exam finished caused the person to decrease their rate of study behavior? If not, how would you go about collecting data that would allow you to infer a causal relation?

EXPERIMENTAL DILEMMA

A researcher submitted the following work to a journal for publication. Twenty second graders were selected to participate in a remedial reading program based on scores obtained on a general reading skills test given to all children in the school system. The students were chosen because they did not perform as well as their classmates in general reading skills, and it was hoped that the program would improve their reading ability. The program involved individual sessions with a special instructor three hours a week for six weeks. At the end of this period, the test was readministered to the students in the program. Scores were compared with those of children of similar ability from another grammar school in the area who took the test again at the same point in the school year as the children in the remedial program. The results showed no difference between scores for students who had participated in the remedial program and those who had not. Although the researcher wanted to conclude that the program had been ineffective, a reviewer argued that the results could have been due to regression artifacts. Do you agree with the reviewer? Why or why not?

MULTIPLE CHOICE QUESTIONS

_____ 1. Most quasi-experiments involving naturally occurring treatments have a structure similar to

a. small-n AB designs.

b. small-n ABA designs.

c. matched group designs.

d. within-subject designs.

_____ 2. Quasi-experiments in the general form observation-treatment-observation cannot be true reversal designs because

a. most natural treatments have long-term carry-over effects.

b. there is no control condition.

c. the variables are generally confounded.

d. all of the above

_____ 3. One way to obtain a "control" group or condition in case-study research is to

a. employ a time-series design.

b. employ a deviant-case analysis.

c. replicate the research in a controlled laboratory experiment.

d. randomly assign subjects to either the case-study condition or the control condition.

_____ 4. In a time-series analysis we are interested in
   a. consistent patterns of responding across the individuals' life span.
   b. separating changes in behavior that are due to maturation from changes that are due to treatment effects.
   c. determining the relative effect of a treatment as a function of when the treatment was introduced.
   d. changes following introduction of the treatment.

_____ 5. One way to increase internal validity in case study research is to use
   a. deviant case analysis.
   b. nonequivalent control groups.
   c. multiple dependent variables.
   d. all of the above

_____ 6. Which of the following is not a subject variable?
   a. sex of individual
   b. political affiliation
   c. weight
   d. age
   e. all of the above are subject variables

_____ 7. Which of the following represents a quasi-experimental research project?
   a. Memory performance is compared between a group of subjects who study material for 10 minutes versus a group who studies for 20 minutes.
   b. Perception of light flashes is compared between subjects who are dark-adapted and those who are not.
   c. SAT scores are compared for students in private and public schools.
   d. Arousal level is measured as a function of type of music presented to subjects.

_____ 8. Which of the following is true concerning quasi-experimental designs?

    a. they are less powerful than observational studies

    b. they often include subject variables

    c. they involve careful manipulation of experimental variables

    d. they are rarely used in psychological research

_____ 9. Matching

    a. is used in quasi-experiments.

    b. is a way of avoiding confounding of subject variables.

    c. introduces the possibility of regression artifacts.

    d. all of the above

_____10. If a researcher wants to use a research design that employs subject variables, then that researcher will

    a. manipulate the subject variable holding other factors constant.

    b. select subjects who have the chosen characteristics in some varying degree.

    c. select a behavior to measure that will not vary with the subject variable.

    d. both b and c

_____11. In designs that employ subject variables, matching refers to

    a. matching subjects on the subject variables.

    b. matching subjects on the behavioral task that is measured.

    c. matching subjects on the variables that may be confounded with the subject variable.

    d. matching subjects on variables that are known to be confounded with the behavioral task.

_____12. The phenomenon of regression to the mean implies that if two abnormally tall parents have a child, the child's adult height will likely be

a. shorter than the mean of the parents' heights.

b. taller than the mean of the parents' heights.

c. close to the mean of the parents' heights.

d. either a or c

_____13. A synergistic relationship among two variables indicates that

a. the two variables interact.

b. the two variables are correlated.

c. the two variables are confounded.

d. both a and c

_____14. Given that age is a subject variable,

a. it may be directly manipulated in an experimental design.

b. it is easy to attribute causation to the age factor as opposed to any other factor in an experimental design.

c. it is examined largely in correlational studies rather than in experimental designs.

d. it may only be treated as a control variable in developmental research.

_____15. A researcher interested in the long-term effects of nuclear wastes monitors the health of 15 families living near a waste disposal site. The researcher records any instance of physical or mental illness reported by the families over a period of 10 years. This sort of study is called a _____ design.

a. cross-sectional

b. cross-sequential

c. longitudinal

d. time-lag

_____16. In a longitudinal design

    a. the confoundings inherent in cross-sectional designs are avoided.

    b. results may be produced by historical events occurring during the course of the study.

    c. the same group of subjects are repeatedly tested as they grow older.

    d. all of the above

_____17. Cross-sequential research designs

    a. allow for causal inferences concerning the effects of subject variables.

    b. confound age with other subject variables of interest.

    c. are much more difficult to run than longitudinal studies.

    d. all of the above

TRUE - FALSE QUESTIONS

_____ 1. Ex post facto analysis involving more than one dependent variable may be interpreted in a causal fashion.

_____ 2. Quasi-experiments of the general form observation-treatment-observation can best be considered a reversal, or ABA design.

_____ 3. Two threats to internal validity with naturally occurring treatments are the history of the subject and changes in the subject that occur over time.

_____ 4. In a nonequivalent control group, matching is attempted after the occurrence of the treatment.

_____ 5. An interrupted-time-series design is the best design that can be used when the size of the effect of the treatment is expected to be delayed for some period.

_____ 6. Ability to recall dreams is an example of a subject variable.

_____ 7. When manipulating a subject variable it is important to hold all other factors constant.

_____ 8. Studies involving subject variables essentially produce correlations between variables.

_____ 9. Matching subjects on relevant variables avoids problems caused by confounding.

_____10. Regression procedures often lead to matching artifacts.

_____11. In a synergistic relationship the two variables exhibit additive effects.

_____12. Matching often reduces the size of the sample on which observations are made.

_____13. Matched variables are rarely under direct control.

_____14. Regression to the mean refers to the phenomenon whereby if people who receive extreme scores on some characteristic are retested, their second scores tend to be closer to the group mean than were their first scores.

_____15. In a cross-sectional research design, the same subjects are repeatedly tested over the course of several years.

_____16. Longitudinal and cross-sectional studies can produce different results due to the fact that age may be confounded with other factors in cross-sectional designs.

_____17. The confounding inherent in cross-sequential designs is eliminated in longitudinal studies.

_____18. Longitudinal designs tend to confound age with other subject variables.

_____19. Time-lag designs determine the effects of time of testing while holding age constant.

_____20. Cross-sequential designs include both longitudinal and cross-sectional components.

ESSAY QUESTIONS

1. In what sense is it meaningful to compare interpreting a case history and doing detective work?

2. Describe briefly the ways in which the internal validity of case studies may be increased.

3. Describe briefly problems associated with the use of age as a subject variable. How might these problems be avoided?

4. What is a cross-sequential design? How is it an improvement over other research designs employing subject variables?

CHAPTER 10.

Guarding Against Threats to Validity

SUMMARY

The results obtained from a research project can be
contaminated by reactivity. Behavior is often influenced by
interactions between the researcher and the participants as well
as by the social and physical setting in which the research is
conducted. A part of the problem is that people may respond
differently when they think they are being observed than they
would under normal conditions. Furthermore, there may be large
differences between the type of person who volunteers for an
experiment and those people who resist such an opportunity. If
the scientifically observed behavior is not characteristic, the
research loses external validity. Sometimes, researchers can
guard against the effects of reactivity by using unobtrusive
observations and measures. In other cases, they attempt to
design experimental procedures, such as "blinding", and select
independent variables that obviate the problems of response
style and subject selection issues.

There is also the possibility that the researcher may
(consciously or unconsciously) affect the outcome of a research
project. Science guards against deliberate research bias
effects by replicating important studies. Failure to replicate

a finding is one of the ways in which science proceeds as a self-correcting enterprise. Inadvertent research bias effects are probably more widespread than deliberate bias. Great care must be taken to try to avoid introducing such inadvertent effects, since they only serve to contaminate the results.

Operational definitions are used in science so that scientists can communicate in a precise manner regarding the constructs they study. An operational definition allows other scientists to replicate the conditions under which observations were made originally.

Because experiments employ rather artificial conditions, a number of scientists have questioned the ecological validity of laboratory experiments. The appropriate concern here is not with mundane realism but rather whether the results obtained in the laboratory generalize to other (real-world) settings. Research has shown that often results from the laboratory do in fact generalize quite well.

KEY TERMS

anthropomorphizing	negativistic-subject role
apprehensive-subject role	operational definition
blind experiment	participant observation
deception	placebo
demand characteristics	random sample
double-blind design	reactivity
ecological validity	realism
evaluation apprehension	researcher bias
faithful-subject role	response acquiescence
field research	response deviation
forced-choice tests	response styles or sets
generalizability	retrospective
good-subject role	reversibility
Hawthorne effect	setting representativeness
motivated forgetting	simulated experiment

social desirability

subject representativeness

subject roles

unobtrusive measures

unobtrusive observations

variable representativeness

volunteer problem

PROGRAMMED REVIEW

1. When the process of observing behavior changes that behavior, the process is said to be _____.

2. Two general ways to guard against participant's reactions from ruining our research is to make unobtrusive _____ or make unobtrusive _____.

3. Unobtrusive measures are _____ observations of behavior.

4. Much of the evidence in a case study is _____ in nature.

5. A problem inherent in case studies is _____ _____: People often distort unpleasant events.

6. Tests and survey results may be contaminated by response _____ or _____ sets.

7. The forced-choice technique used in Edwards' Personal Preference Schedule is designed to minimize contamination caused by _____ _____.

8. One problem inherent in interpreting data from opinion surveys that rely on volunteer mailings is the _____ _____.

9. A well known example of participant reaction is the _____ _____, named after a study in which industrial workers participated in a long experiment.

10. The Hawthorne effect represents one kind of _____.

11. A subject who adopts a _____ _____ role will do anything necessary to validate the experimental hypothesis.

12. Experiments conducted in natural settings are known as _____.

13. Experiments conducted in natural settings suffer from the fact that the _____ that is characteristic of laboratory experiments may be lost in the natural environment.

14. An experiment in which pertinent information is withheld from the participant is called a _____ _____.

15. Deliberate researcher effects (such as faking data) can be detected through failure to _____ the results.

16. One way to minimize inadvertent differential treatments is to make the researcher _____ with respect to potentially important aspects of the study.

17. When both the researcher and the subject are uninformed about important aspects of the study, this is called a _____-_____ design.

18. A pharmacologically inert substance is known as a _____.

19. Attributing human characteristics to animals is called _____.

20. An operational definition is a formula for defining a construct in a way that other scientists can _____.

21. An operational definition does not have to _____ _____ but it must be stated so that it can be _____.

22. If a process cannot be directly _____ but must instead be inferred, then that process should be tied to _____.

23. When we link our operational definitions we help make them more _____.

24. Research psychologists try to understand the _____ that underlie behavior.

25. The ability to generalize across different experimental manipulations is called _____ _____.

26.   _____ refers to whether the experimental setting bears a resemblance to the real world.

27.   To test the generalizability of experimental results we might repeat the observations in a _____ _____.

28.   Concern with ecological validity should be with the psychological _____ being studied.

EXPERIMENTAL PROJECT

In this project you will examine the problem of reactivity in experimentation. In this project one half of your participants will not be aware that he or she is being observed. Therefore it is <u>your responsibility</u> to ensure that the potential gains from conducting this project exceed any potential harm that might be done to your participants. Actually, there is very little risk of any harm to your participants but, nonetheless, it is your responsibility to ensure that (a) you are reasonably certain that this project is safe for your participants, and (b) that after completing the project you discuss with your subject what this project was about.

The design of this project is straightforward. You are going to ask people to perform some innocuous task, such as telling you how many windows there are in their house or apartment. Tell half of your participants that you are curious about whatever task it is that you request them to perform. Tell the remaining people in your sample that you are conducting an experimental demonstration as part of your psychology class. Your dependent variable will be what percentage of people are willing to comply with your request.

Was there any difference in the rate of responding for your two groups? How do you think that people would have behaved if you brought them into a psychology laboratory and asked them to perform this task?

EXPERIMENTAL DILEMMA

A researcher interested in group dynamics hypothesizes that if groups of subjects are given a problem to solve, they will be able to reach a unanimous consensus sooner if the group is composed totally of members of the same sex. She proposes the following design. Groups of either six males, six females, or three males and three females will meet in a conference room. The researcher (who will test all of the subjects herself) will give the subjects the resumes of three people who are being considered for a supervisory position in a shipping company. The group's task will be to choose one of the applicants through discussion and deliberation. The experimenter will be present and will act as a moderator but will not attempt to sway the decision one way or another. The amount of time needed to reach a decision will be compared between groups composed of either the same sex or difference sexes. Are there any problems in the proposed procedure? If so, what are they?

MULTIPLE CHOICE QUESTIONS

_____ 1. Unobtrusive measures are
    a. direct observations taken without the awareness of the individual(s) being observed.
    b. indirect observations of behavior.
    c. obtained through participant observation.
    d. best avoided in naturalistic observations.

_____ 2. Which of the following does not pose a problem when attempting to interpret the results of a case study?
    a. the evidence is retrospective
    b. memory is fallible
    c. incomplete records
    d. none of the above

_____ 3. Which of the following is not a type of response style?

    a. response acquiescence

    b. response deviation

    c. social adaptability

    d. social desirability

_____ 4. Edwards' Personal Preference Schedule employs a forced choice test procedure in an effort to

    a. avoid response-style problems.

    b. avoid motivated forgetting.

    c. solve the volunteer problem.

    d. remove demand characteristics.

_____ 5. Subject reactivity refers to the problem of

    a. subjects misinterpreting the experimenter's instructions.

    b. the influence of the expectations of the experimenter on the experimental results.

    c. the subjects' behavior being influenced by being in an experiment.

    d. treatment carryover effects.

_____ 6. Reactivity can be minimized in observational research by

    a. using a double-blind procedure.

    b. using unobtrusive measures.

    c. employing a placebo.

    d. participant observation.

_____ 7. Response style refers to

    a. demand characteristics in field research.

    b. reconstructive processes in retrospective memory.

    c. a habitual way of answering a question.

    d. a source of reactivity in interviewing and surveys.

    e. both c and d

_____ 8. The "volunteer problem" refers to

    a. the problem associated with getting people to participate in psychological experiments.

    b. people who volunteer differ in many ways from people who do not volunteer.

    c. the ethics of using volunteers in experimentation.

    d. identifying a sample of people who are likely to volunteer for an experiment.

_____ 9. In order to be able to generalize the results of your research to the general population, you should

    a. conduct field research to validate laboratory research.

    b. use a forced choice procedure in testing.

    c. avoid using volunteer subjects.

    d. maximize the social desirability of responding.

    e. assign subject to conditions using a random procedure.

_____10. The nonrespondent problem in survey research can be solved by

    a. obtaining a random sample of the entire available population.

    b. using a random sample of the respondents.

    c. matching respondents and nonrespondents.

    d. avoiding the possibility of response style affecting results by using a forced choice procedure.

_____11. In studies involving correlational measures

    a. response style is generally not a problem.

    b. demand characteristics are less evident than in laboratory studies.

    c. participants often respond according to their perceptions of the project.

    d. volunteer problems are unlikely to affect the outcome.

_____12. The Hawthorne Effect is a classic example of
   a. participant reaction in an experiment.
   b. experimenter bias.
   c. field research using unobtrusive measures.
   d. mistakenly inferring causation from a correlation.

_____13. The Orne and Evans (1965) study involving asking subjects to perform dangerous acts demonstrates
   a. social conformity.
   b. a lack of ecological validity.
   c. unethical research.
   d. the volunteer problem.
   e. demand characteristics.

_____14. Which of the following is not a social role described by Weber and Cook (1972)?
   a. apprehensive-subject role
   b. faithful-subject
   c. good-subject role
   d. negativistic-subject role
   e. none of the above

_____15. One advantage of field experiments over laboratory experiments is that in field experiments there is
   a. less of a volunteer problem.
   b. less of a chance of violating ethics due to the use of unobtrusive measures.
   c. less risk of demand characteristics due to the use of unobtrusive measures.
   d. a wider range of behaviors that can be observed.

_____16. Unobtrusive measures can be used in a laboratory experiment by using
   a. deception.
   b. placebos.
   c. double-blind techniques.
   d. retrospective measures.
   e. simulated experiments.

_____17. In a blind experiment

   a. the experimenter does not directly observe the subjects behavior.

   b. the participant is unaware that an experiment is taking place.

   c. some pertinent information is withheld from the subject.

   d. demand characteristics may actually increase.

_____18. In a simulated experiment

   a. the demands of the situation are assumed to be the same for participants in all conditions.

   b. a laboratory experiment is replicated in an environment created to simulate the real world.

   c. there is greater ecological validity than in a laboratory experiment.

   d. both b and c

_____19. Inadvertent researcher effects can be minimized by

   a. using a double-blind technique.

   b. not allowing the researcher to know which condition subjects have been assigned to.

   c. using a thought experiment.

   d. conducting field experiments.

   e. both a and b

_____20. A placebo is

   a. a pharmacologically inert substance.

   b. used to reduce demand characteristics.

   c. given to subjects in the experimental condition.

   d. all of the above

   e. both a and b

_____21. The most common way for a scientist to provide a technical meaning for a concept is by way of
    a. an operational definition.
    b. a common definition.
    c. a dictionary definition.
    d. a hypothetical construct.
_____22. Ecological validity refers to the ability to generalize research finds to the _____ to which they are intended to apply.
    a. population
    b. people
    c. species
    d. environmental settings
    e. both b and d
_____23. Ecological validity is
    a. more dependent on generalizability than on surface realism.
    b. more dependent on surface realism than on generalizability.
    c. equally dependent on surface realism and generalizability.
    d. does not depend on either surface realism or on generalizability.

TRUE-FALSE QUESTIONS
_____ 1. Demand characteristics refer to subject reactivity.
_____ 2. Unobtrusive observations are usually indirect measures of behavior.
_____ 3. Analysis of discarded garbage and refuse is an example of an unobtrusive measure of behavior.
_____ 4. Research has shown that parents often misremember events concerning their children's early years.

_____ 5. The volunteer problem refers to the difficulty in obtaining a sample of participants for a research project.

_____ 6. In survey research the nonrespondent problem can be solved by obtaining a random sample of those who did not respond and interviewing them.

_____ 7. Demand characteristics might be magnified in correlational research that involves two measures of the people that are taken at the same time.

_____ 8. The Hawthorne Effect is a classic example of demand characteristics.

_____ 9. Field experiments maintain a higher level of control than is possible in a laboratory experiment.

_____ 10. If the results of a simulated experiment are highly similar to the results obtained with the independent variable, we can concluded that the independent variable effectively controls behavior.

_____ 11. Deliberate researcher effects can be detected by direct replications.

_____ 12. Deliberate researcher effects are more difficult to detect than are inadvertent researcher effects.

_____ 13. Anthropomorphism refers to the tendency to attribute animal characteristics to humans.

_____ 14. Results concerning the operation of sensory processes in college students is very likely to generalize to other people.

ESSAY QUESTIONS

1. How may reactivity affect the results of a survey? What procedures can be used to solve this problem?

2. What is a blind experiment? A double-blind experiment? How are these different from a thought experiment?

3. What is an operational definition? How are these useful in psychology?

4. What is ecological validity? How can a researcher increase the ecological validity of his studies?

CHAPTER 11.
Interpreting the Results of Research

SUMMARY

One problem encountered in research is that of scale attenuation. This occurs when performance on a task approaches either end of the scale of measurement. When performance is nearly perfect this is called a ceiling effect and the lack of performance is called a floor effect. It is inappropriate to say that performance is equal in two conditions when performance levels reflect scale attenuation. This is because we have no way of knowing how the two groups might compare if we were able to bring performance levels up or down within the confines of the dependent measure.

Another problem that may affect the interpretation of the results of a study is regression to the mean: Extreme scores obtained during one testing session may be due to measurement error, and thus will regress to the mean of the group upon further testing. Regression artifacts are particularly troublesome when subjects are drawn from different populations and may still persist even when subjects are matched across conditions on other important characteristics.

When we are confronted with the results of psychological research we must ask whether they are reliable and valid. One way to determine the reliability of a pattern of results is to replicate the original study. This may be done either by a direct replication in which the original study is repeated as closely as possible or by a systematic or conceptual replication, in which some aspect of the original methodology is changed.

Quite often in psychological research there exists more than one possible explanation for an experimental finding. When this happens researchers are well advised to use converging operations in which one explanation is arrived at through more than one path of research. Such a strategy was used in determining the loci of the personal space and Stroop effects.

KEY TERMS

ceiling effects	regression artifact
conceptual replication	regression to the mean
converging operations	replication
direct replication	scale-attenuation effects
Einstellung	Stroop effect
experimental reliability	systematic replication
floor effects	test reliability
personal space	

PROGRAMMED REVIEW

1. Performance levels near either to the top or the bottom of the scale of the dependent variable are called _____-_____ effects.

2. _____ effects are observed when performance is almost perfect and _____ effects are observed when performance is almost nonexistent.

3. Scarborough found that recall was higher in the _____ presentation condition than in the _____ presentation condition.

4. Scarborough's data showed evidence of a _____ effect at the zero-second retention interval.

5. Researchers usually test small groups of _____ subjects to determine whether ceiling or floor effects are going to be a problem in their research.

6. If a scale attenuation problem exists, then one way to avoid this problem is to change the task _____.

7. If people are given two successive tests and we find that those who scored high on test 1 tended to score somewhat lower on test 2, this would represent a statistical _____ to the _____.

8. Regression artifacts occur because all psychological measures are subject to a certain amount of _____.

9. In the Westinghouse-Ohio study the two samples of children probably came from different _____.

10. The best method for eliminating confounding factors is _____ _____ of subjects to conditions.

11. Two key factors for ensuring reliability are a _____ number of observations and a _____ result.

12. An unreliable test is also an _____ test.

13. Many experimental psychologists find _____ reliability more convincing than statistical reliability.

14. In Luchins' water jar problem the (experimental/control) _____ group received all 11 problems to solve.

15. In a _____ _____ an experiment is repeated as closely as possible with as few changes as possible in the method.

16. In a _____ replication many factors that the investigator considers irrelevant to the phenomenon of interest are changed in the replication.

17. _____ _____ are a set of two or more operations that eliminate alternative concepts that might explain a set of experimental results.

18. In a(n) _____ task subjects are required to name the color of ink that a word is printed in.

19. The Stroop effect is an (increase/decrease) of the time needed to name the color of ink used to spell the name of a different color.

20. By using converging operations, Egeth, Blecker and Kamlet (1969) showed that the Stroop effect is due to _____ _____ and not to _____ _____.

21. In Kinzel's (1970) study on personal space, the dependent variable was

_____

_____

22. Barefoot, Hoople and McClay (1972) found that _____ people stopped to drink water when the experimenter sat close to the fountain than when he sat far from the fountain.

EXPERIMENTAL PROJECT

Luchins's (1942) water-jar problems have been studied extensively and Luchins's original results have been found to be highly reliable. In this project you can determine whether the same results would be obtained under conditions in which the problem solver is under time pressure. Specifically, will the group of subjects who write "Don't be blind" prior to problem 7 (see text page 237) show less of an Einstellung effect than the experimental group when they are trying to solve the problem as rapidly as possible? To test this hypothesis conduct a replication of Luchins' original demonstration, as described on pages 237-238 of the text. Tell half of your subjects that you are going to time their problem solving, and that they should work as quickly as possible. Do not mention this to the remaining subjects.

Did the time-pressure subjects show the same pattern of results as the no time-pressure group? What do these results indicate about the generality of Luchins' results?

EXPERIMENTAL DILEMMA

A researcher working for the Defense Department wanted to determine whether pilots or air traffic controllers were more affected by environmental stress. The researcher selected a task known as a speech shadowing task to answer this question. In a speech shadowing task two different messages are presented to the subjects, one in each ear (i.e., a dichotic message) and the subjects' task is to repeat aloud (shadow) the message presented in one ear.

Ten pilots and 10 air traffic controllers were selected for the experiment. The subjects were matched on age, years in their respective occupations, and sex. Each group of subjects shadowed a dichotic message under two conditions, a high stress condition and a low stress condition. Subjects received 20 trials under each condition in an ABBA design. Each trial consists of the presentation of five different items to both the attended and the unattended ear. The subjects' task is to shadow one message (the attended message), and when the message is completed to try and recall the items presented to the unattended ear. Items are presented at the rate of one item pair per second. The assignment of items to the unattended and attended ear is completely counterbalanced across subjects and conditions.

The dependent variable is the number of items recalled from the nonattended ear. The mean number of items recalled in each condition was as follows:

	Stress Condition	
Subjects	Low Stress	High Stress
Pilots	97%	80%
Controllers	98%	94%

A statistical analysis revealed that the interaction of level of stress (high vs. low) and type of subject (pilot vs. controller) was significant at the .01 level of significance. The main effect of type of subject was also significant ($p < .05$).

Because there was an interaction effect the researcher concluded that the pilots were more affected by stress than were the controllers, although this difference was only present in the high stress condition. Under low stress conditions the two groups were equally affected by stress.

Do you agree or disagree with this conclusion? Why or why not? How would _you_ design an experiment to test whether pilots or controllers are more affected by stress?

MULTIPLE CHOICE QUESTIONS

_____ 1. Scale attenuation effects are observed when
   a. subjects fail to show any savings from one learning trial to the next.
   b. performance is virtually perfect or virtually nonexistent.
   c. recognition performance is superior to recall performance.
   d. recency effects are larger than primary effects.

_____ 2. Scarborough (1972) could not draw any conclusions about differential forgetting in his auditory and visual retention presentation conditions because

a. performance in the auditory and visual presentation conditions was equivalent across all retention intervals.

b. performance was virtually perfect in all conditions at the zero retention interval.

c. performance was poorer in the auditory than in the visual presentation condition at the longer retention intervals.

d. performance was poorer in the visual than in the auditory presentation at the longer retention intervals.

_____ 3. Which of the following statements best summarizes the problem of scale attenuation effects?

a. There is no such thing as perfectly good or perfectly bad performance.

b. The size of the intervals of a dependent measure are unequal when you approach the extreme ends of the scale.

c. It is impossible to determine whether there are differences among experimental conditions when performance is polarized at either the high or low end of the scale of the dependent measure.

d. Most of the dependent measures used to study memory are relatively unconstrained and thus allow for easy interpretation of performance levels.

_____ 4. One might reduce problems of ceiling and floor effects by

   a. avoiding the use of tasks that are too easy.

   b. avoiding the use of tasks that are too difficult.

   c. testing pilot subjects to make sure that performance on a task will not be near the extremes of the scale.

   d. all of the above

_____ 5. Statistical regression to the mean refers to the fact that

   a. when people are tested twice, those with high scores on test 1 tend to have scores that are closer to the group mean on test 2.

   b. in psychology most test scores tend to fall close to the mean, with few very deviant scores.

   c. in an experiment employing repeated tests, subjects who perform poorly on the early test(s) will tend to do better on the later test(s).

   d. both a and c

_____ 6. Quasi-experimental designs are particularly susceptible to bias due to measurement error because

   a. there are no control variables.

   b. subjects are not randomly assigned to groups.

   c. the experimental and control groups are not matched prior to the introduction of the independent variable.

   d. all of the above

_____ 7. Two students take a History exam. The first student has an A average but makes a C on the test whereas the second student who had a D average makes an A on the exam. Assuming that these discrepancies are due to measurement error, it is likely that the first student will make a(n) _____ and the second student will make a(n) _____ on the next exam.

    a. C; A

    b. A; C

    c. C; C

    d. C; B

_____ 8. The reliability of a test refers to

    a. whether the test measures what it is intended to measure.

    b. how well the test can predict future performance.

    c. how stable scores are across testings of the same subjects.

    d. how stable scores are across different groups.

_____ 9. The basic issue regarding reliability of experimental results is:

    a. whether we can draw a conclusion regarding a causal relation between the independent and dependent variables.

    b. if the experiment were repeated would the results be the same as were found the first time.

    c. whether the conclusions are warranted, given the design of the experiment.

    d. the presence or absence of possible confounding factors.

_____ 10. Einstellung is the German word for _____.

    a. problem

    b. experimentation

    c. reactivity

    d. set

_____11. In a _____ we replicate a phenomenon or concept, but in a way that differs from the original demonstration.

    a. systematic replication

    b. paradigmatic replication

    c. conceptual replication

    d. indirect replication

_____12. Converging operations

    a. are a set of two or more operations used to eliminate alternative explanations for a set of experimental results.

    b. provide more than one way of arriving at an experimental conclusion.

    c. allow psychologists to distinguish between two competing explanations of an effect.

    d. all of the above

_____13. Which of the following is true?

    a. Converging operations are useful in validating mental constructs.

    b. Converging operations are experimental operations that produce different results.

    c. Converging operations are a set of two or more operational definitions.

    d. both a and c.

_____14. The Stroop effect is a phenomenon in which the time required to name the color of the ink a word is printed in _____ when the word is the name of a color other than the ink as opposed to a neutral word.

    a. increases

    b. decreases

    c. remains constant

    d. increases for warm colors and decreases for cool colors

_____15. The results of the Egeth, Blecker and Kamlet (1969) experiment indicate that the Stroop effect has its influence on the _____ portion of the task.

    a. perceptual

    b. input

    c. inhibition

    d. response

_____16. The most important reason for a psychologist to use converging operations is to

    a. support inferences about processes that cannot be directly inferred.

    b. replicate an experimental finding to ensure its reliability.

    c. increase precision of the dependent variable.

    d. define a process in terms of its operations.

_____17. Prisoners were found to have larger personal space bubbles when they were classified as

    a. nonviolent.

    b. violent.

    c. depressed.

    d. homosexual.

_____18. Kinzel (1970) found that violent prisoners have

    a. larger personal space bubbles than nonviolent prisoners.

    b. smaller personal space bubbles than nonviolent prisoners.

    c. a larger personal space area in front than in behind.

    d. both a and c

_____19. In approaching a violent prisoner, you would be more likely to invade his personal space if you approached from the prisoner's
    a. left side.
    b. right side.
    c. front.
    d. rear.

TRUE-FALSE QUESTIONS

_____ 1. Based on Scarborough's (1972) results we can conclude that forgetting is greater for auditory than for visual presentation.

_____ 2. There is no way to avoid ceiling and floor effects in psychological research; we just have to learn to interpret them carefully.

_____ 3. A typical finding is that recall is better for auditory than for visual presentation.

_____ 4. Scarborough (1972) concluded that his results indicated that the rate of forgetting is greater for information presented through the ears than through the eyes.

_____ 5. Scale attenuation effects can hide actual differences that may exist between experimental conditions.

_____ 6. Scale attenuation effects can be avoided by effectively manipulating task difficulty.

_____ 7. Regression to the mean is an experimental artifact.

_____ 8. Regression artifacts would never be a problem if measurement error could be eliminated completely.

_____ 9. Regression artifacts pose very few problems as long as subjects are drawn from different underlying populations.

_____10. Quasi-experimental designs are less susceptible to bias than true experiments because of regression to the mean.

_____11. If a test is reliable then we know that it measures what it was intended to measure.

_____12. Many psychologists find experimental reliability less convincing than statistical reliability.

_____13. A direct replication involves simply repeating an experiment as closely as possible with as few changes in the method as possible.

_____14. Kinzel (1970) found that violent prisoners have larger personal space "bubbles" than do nonviolent prisoners.

_____15. Converging operations are a set of two or more operations that suggest alternative explanations for an experimental result.

_____16. The general finding in the Stroop task is that the time required to name ink color decreases when the stimulus word is the name of a color other than the ink it is printed in.

_____17. Using converging operations, Egeth, Blecker and Kamlet (1969) showed that interference in the Stroop task was localized in the response system.

_____18. An experimenter can be satisfied that he or she has eliminated all alternative explanations of an experimental result if two converging operations have led to the same conclusion.

ESSAY QUESTIONS

1. Define and give an example of scale attenuation effects. Why are these effects problematic? How might a researcher avoid these problems?

2. What are converging operations? Describe how converging operations were used to discover the focus of the Stroop effect.

3. What is meant by regression to the mean? Can this problem arise only with a within-subject design or could it also arise when a between-subject design is employed? How might such regression effects affect the interpretation of experimental results?

CHAPTER 12.
Conducting Ethical Research

SUMMARY

This chapter discusses the problems of ethical considerations in psychological research involving human and animal subjects. A basic theme stressed throughout the chapter is that an ethical researcher does everything in his or her power to protect the physical and mental well-being of research participants. To aid psychologists in maintaining ethical standards, the American Psychological Association publishes guidelines for ethical considerations in research. Portions of these guidelines are reproduced in the text.

Research involving the use of human subjects requires that the research participants (or an appropriate representative of the person) give informed consent to participate in the research. Informed consent means that the research is explained to the person in sufficient detail so as to allow the person to make a reasonable judgement about whether to participate. Participants must always be allowed to decline to participate in the research or to withdraw at any time.

Subjects should be debriefed at the end of the research project, which means that the investigator explains the general purposes of the research and the nature of the manipulations used. The investigator must strive to remove any misconceptions that may have arisen as a result of participating in the experiment. All data collected in the experiment must remain confidential, unless otherwise agreed. Often times the goal of upholding these various ethical principles results in a dilemma in that upholding one principle may violate another.

Investigators employing animals as subjects must do everything possible to ensure that the animals are treated in a humane fashion. While there is considerable debate concerning the use of animals in research, many scientists (including the authors) would argue that animal research is essential for scientific progress. Nonetheless, it is important that researchers continue to strive to treat animals in as humane a fashion as possible.

Finally, research with drugs poses another whole set of ethical problems. Besides considerations concerning the welfare of the subjects while they are participating in the research, the investigator must also provide appropriate aftercare for the subjects. Drug research also requires that the investigator conform with various legal requirements concerning the use of drugs in research.

KEY TERMS

aftercare

confidentiality

debriefing

deception

freedom to withdraw

informed consent

Institutional Review Board

protection from harm

removing harmful consequences

speciesism

PROGRAMMED REVIEW

1. Most universities and research institutions have _____ committees that judge the ethicality of proposed research.

2. Individuals should read and understand the ethical principles of the American Psychological Association _____ they conduct a research project with human participants.

3. Subjects should be warned ahead of time if there is any potential _____ that might result from participating in the experiment.

4. The experimenter is obliged to _____ any harm that threatens the subject.

5. Psychologists who conduct research with human participants are obliged to respect the _____ and _____ of the participants in the research.

6. Individuals must be given the option of _____ from the research at any time.

7. The investigator must protect both the _____ and the _____ state of his or her subjects.

8. If a researcher divulges too many details of an experiment this could result in a(n) _____ invalid research project.

9. When students taking an introductory psychology course are required to participate in experiments as part of a course requirement, they should have some _____ way of fulfilling this requirement.

10. _____ means that the experimenter explains the general purposes of the research and the nature of the manipulations used.

11. Unless otherwise agreed, what a subject does in an experiment should be _____.

12. Ethical decisions are rarely made on the basis of _____ facts.

13. _____ is a form of racism involving claims about scientific progress being helped by animal research.

14. Animal subjects should be treated humanely, and the decision to inflict pain on an animal should be based on a weighing of the _____ and _____ of the research.

15. As a model for _____ and _____ behavior, animal research is essential for scientific progress.

EXPERIMENTAL PROJECT

This project is designed to get you to consider in more detail the issues of ethics in research. Make up a short list of experiments that you think are in some way unethical, but that you might like to perform just to see what happens. Visit faculty members who specialize in the research areas of your experiments and ask them if they would be willing to supervise the experiments.

Did the faculty members question the ethics of your proposed experiment? How many faculty members told you that they refuse because the proposed research is unethical? How many tried to see if there might be a way to answer the question posed in your research, but using an ethical experiment? Finally, after reading the issues raised in the chapter, would you consider this to be an ethical project? Why or why not?

EXPERIMENTAL DILEMMA

A social psychologist is interested in studying how decisions are made concerning ethics in research by peer evaluation committees. In other words, she wants to study the university committee that decides whether or not a proposed research project conforms to conventional ethical standards. The problem confronted by this research is that she needs to get the approval of this committee before she can study them.

Is it possible to conduct internally and externally valid research on this issue? What ethical problems might the research face? How could she avoid demand characteristics, or reactivity, from affecting her results? Assume for the moment that one of the ways this psychologist intends to study the decision-making process is to submit fake research proposals under the name of another (consenting) researcher. Some of these proposals would violate ethical standards, others would not. Is this an ethical approach? How might you design a research project to address the problem of interest (i.e., the decision-making process)?

MULTIPLE CHOICE QUESTIONS

_____ 1. The principle of informed consent means that the researcher has an obligation to
   a. submit all research proposals to a peer committee that will judge the ethics of the proposed research.
   b. tell subjects prior to participation all aspects of the research that might reasonably be expected to influence willingness to participate.
   c. only disclose the results of the experiment after he has obtained the consent of all subjects who participated in the study.
   d. agree to perform the research only after he or she is certain that no ethical standards are being violated.

_____ 2. In an ethical research project
   a. informed consent is obtained from all participants.
   b. participants may withdraw at any time.
   c. the potential gains outweigh the potential harm.
   d. all of the above
   e. both a and b

_____ 3. In the Elmes, et al study on depression and memory
   a. the researchers did not deceive the participants.
   b. both the experimental and control group received depression induction.
   c. subjects in the control group responded as if they were depressed.
   d. participants were given a list of people to contact if the depression continued.

_____ 4. One problem associated with providing enough information for informed consent is that
   a. the validity of the experimental design may be undermined.
   b. people may avoid participating in all psychology research, even low-risk studies.
   c. some research projects may not be able to obtain subjects.
   d. it is a time-consuming process.

_____ 5. Debriefing means that
   a. the investigator is aware of the potential risks involved is the experiment.
   b. the investigator explains the general purpose of the research after the study is completed.
   c. the investigator provides the ethics committee with an abstract of each proposed research project.
   d. after a blind experiment is run the investigator tells the research assistants what the purpose of the experiment was.

_____ 6. Animals are often used as subjects in psychological research because

    a. ethical considerations are generally less stringent with animal research than with human research.

    b. they are interesting.

    c. they form an important part of the natural world.

    d. all of the above

    e. both b and c

_____ 7. Singer (1978) calls claims about scientific progress being helped by animal research

    a. anthropomorphism.

    b. explicitly unethical.

    c. speciesism.

    d. unfounded.

    e. all of the above

TRUE - FALSE QUESTIONS

_____ 1. Any federally funded research must be approved by an ethics review committee before any funding is granted.

_____ 2. In a research project, every member of the research team is responsibile for ensuring ethical practice in research.

_____ 3. In the Elmes, et al (1984) study on the effect of depression on memory, subjects were told about the possible side effects of the depressant drug during the debriefing session.

_____ 4. Providing information for informed consent generally helps reduce the reactivity of the experimental design.

_____ 5. Participants are always allowed to withdraw from an experiment regardless of their reasons for withdrawing.

_____ 6. Informed consent is generally obtained in writing during the debriefing session.

_____ 7. Confidentiality means that, in general, results of an experiment are not published unless the subject gives his or her approval.

_____ 8. Ethical decisions are never made on the basis of pragmatic concerns.

ESSAY QUESTIONS

1. Under what circumstances (if any) might an ethics review committee allow an experiment involving deception to be conducted?

2. Describe in your own words the argument used in the textbook to argue in favor of animal research.

3. What is meant by aftercare? How would this concept relate to the famous Milgram studies on obedience in which participants though they were giving electric shocks to another person?

CHAPTER 13.
Reading and Writing Research Reports

SUMMARY

To derive the most information from reading an article it is important that you read critically. Each of the sections of a basic psychology article (the title and authors, abstract, introduction, method, results, discussion and references) contains information that is useful in either deciding whether or not to read the article or in evaluating the article and the research reported in the article.

The chapter presents a checklist for critical readers. This checklist is designed to help you as you begin to read and evaluate articles in psychological journals and to get into the habit of actively asking questions about the reports you read. These questions are also useful when you write your own research reports.

Writing and trying to publish the results of a research projects can be a long and tedious task. However, it is important that the results of carefully done research projects are communicated to others who are interested in the problem being studied.

KEY TERMS

abstract	method
APA format	procedure
apparatus	references
author	running head
checklist for critical readers	subjects
discussion	tables
figures	title
introduction	

PROGRAMMED REVIEW

1. The seven parts of a basic psychology article are:

   (a)_____ and _____

   (b)_____

   (c)_____

   (d)_____

   (e)_____

   (f)_____

   (g)_____

2. The format of journal articles in psychology is governed by the _____ _____ of the American Psychological Association.

3. Most titles state the _____ and _____ variables.

4. The _____ is a short paragraph that summarizes the key points of the article.

5. The references are found at the _____ of an article.

6. The Introduction should specify the _____ to be studied, the _____ to be tested and the rationale behind any _____.

7. If you wanted to replicate an experiment you would need to consult the _____ section in the article that describes the experiment.

8. The Method section is sometimes divided up into three subsections that cover: _____, _____, and _____.

9. The _____ section contains a summary of what happened in the experiment.

10. If different figures are included in an article it is important to check that the _____ are comparable so that effects can be compared across figures.

11. Extra skepticism (on the part of the reader) is required when reading the _____ section.

12. In the Introduction section the _____ is usually obvious and clearly stated, while the author's _____ may sometimes have to be inferred.

13. Before you read the Method section you should try to design an _____ to test the _____ stated in the Introduction.

14. After you have read the Method section you should check to see that the methods used are adequate for testing the _____.

15. You should try to predict the results for the experiment before reading the _____ section.

16. In an APA-style report, the cover sheet includes

    _____

    _____

17. Page two of a research report contains the _____.

18. The title of a research project appears on the _____-_____ and immediately precedes the _____ section.

19. Any published reports cited in a paper are listed in the _____.

20. The biggest stylistic problem in most research reports is _____ from one section to the next.

21. The _____ tense should be used in the Introduction and Method section and the _____ tense is generally acceptable for the Results and Discussion sections.

EXPERIMENTAL PROJECT

The best way to get good at reading journal articles is through practice. The more articles you read the more proficient you will become at reading reports. Each time you read an article you should try to answer all of the suggested questions for critical readers (listed in Table 13-1). For further practice reading journal articles, consult your university library. The Bulletin of the Psychonomic Society is a good source for articles to practice reading, since there is a page limit for the articles that appear in that journal. Finally, it is a good idea to get together with classmates and decide upon one or more articles to read. After you have read the articles(s) and written out your answers to the questions in Table 13-1, you should compare you answers with your classmates.

MULTIPLE CHOICE QUESTIONS

_____ 1. Each of the following is a part of a journal article except the _____.
   a. introduction
   b. method
   c. results
   d. discussion
   e. summary

_____ 2. In the "Introduction" of a journal article the author should
   a. specify the problem to be studied.
   b. specify the hypothesis (or hypotheses) to be tested.
   c. give the rationale behind any predictions.
   d. all of the above

_____ 3. Which of the following should be included in the "Method" section of a journal article?

a. considerations concerning subjects

b. a description of the apparatus used in the experiment

c. the procedure of the experiment

d. all of the above

e. both a and b

_____ 4. Which of the following would be unusual to find in the "Results" section of a journal article?

a. raw data

b. summary statistics

c. inferential statistics

d. the level of significance

_____ 5. The interpretation of the experimental findings is found in the _____.

a. abstract

b. introduction

c. method

d. results

e. discussion

_____ 6. The question "What hypothesis will be tested?" should be answered by reading the _____.

a. abstract

b. introduction

c. method

d. results

e. discussion

_____ 7. The question "What is the independent variable?" should
be answered by reading the _____.

a. abstract

b. introduction

c. method

d. results

e. discussion

_____ 8. The question "Are the results expected?" should be
answered by reading the _____.

a. abstract

b. introduction

c. method

d. results

e. discussion

_____ 9. The question "Is my interpretation better than the
author's?" should be answered by reading the _____.

a. abstract

b. introduction

c. method

d. results

e. discussion

_____10. In preparing a lab report or a journal article, you
should use headings for all of the major sections of
the paper <u>except</u> the _____.

a. abstract

b. introduction

c. method

d. results

e. discussion

TRUE - FALSE QUESTIONS

_____ 1. The introduction of a journal article specifies the
hypothesis to be studied and briefly describes the
experiment designed to test the hypothesis.

_____ 2. Statistical design features of an experiment are described in the "Method" section of a journal article.

_____ 3. The statement "$\underline{F}(6,20) = 7.40, p = .01$" means that the odds for obtaining an $\underline{F}$-statistic at least as large as 7.40 by chance if the experiment were repeated would be one percent.

_____ 4. In the "Discussion" section of a journal article, the author is free to interpret the results, and thus the reader must accept the author's interpretation.

_____ 5. The most important question for the reader to answer after reading the "Method" section is: Is this how I would design an experiment to test this hypothesis?

_____ 6. It is appropriate to use the past tense in the review of other studies in the introduction.

_____ 7. Blind reviewing refers to a review of a manuscript where the reviewer does not know the identity of the author(s).

ESSAY QUESTIONS

1. Name the sections of a journal article and briefly describe the function of each section.

2. Why is it important to be wary of statements like "although the improvement observed following training did not quite achieve the level of significance, it is clear that the data reveal a trend in the predicted direction?"

Appendix A
Descriptive Statistics

SUMMARY

An understanding of basic statistical principles is critical to the conduct and interpretation of psychological research. There are two primary branches of statistics that psychologists are concerned with, namely descriptive statistics and inferential statistics. Descriptive statistics are reviewed in Appendix A and inferential statistics are covered in Appendix B.

Descriptive statistics are used to summarize and organize the raw data that is collected in a research project. Descriptive statistics thus provide a way of both systemizing and summarizing the mass of data collected in an experiment or some other type of study. The two primary types of descriptive statistics are measures of central tendency and measures of dispersion. Measures of central tendency indicate the center of the distribution of scores, while measures of dispersion indicate how far the scores are spread out about the center. The primary measure of central tendency is the arithmetic mean of the distribution. The median (the middle-most score) is occasionally used, while the mode (the most frequently occurring score) is rarely used. The two primary measures of dispersion are the standard deviation and variance.

KEY TERMS

arithmetic mean	mean deviation
frequency distribution	measures of central tendency
frequency polygon	measures of dispersion
inflection point	median
mode	standard deviation
normal curve	variance
range	z-scores

PROGRAMMED REVIEW

1. The two main types of descriptive statistics are measures of _____ _____ and measures of _____.

2. One type of graphical representation of numerical data is a _____ or, bar graph.

3. The histogram and the _____ _____ are both examples of _____ distributions.

4. The most common measure of central tendency in psychological research is the _____ _____.

5. The midpoint of the distribution is called the _____ while the most frequently occurring score in the distribution is called the _____.

6. A measure of central tendency that is relatively insensitive to extreme scores is the _____.

7. The difference between the highest and lowest scores in the distribution is called the _____.

8. When calculating the mean deviation, it is necessary to use the _____ value of the difference between each score and the group mean.

9.   The _____ of a distribution is defined as the sum of the squared deviations from the mean divided by the number of scores.

10.   The square root of the variance gives us the _____ _____ of the distribution.

11.   The formula for the variance is:

      s = _____

12.   Psychologists typically present the _____ and the _____ _____ when describing a set of data.

13.   A useful property of the normal curve is that a specific _____ of the scores fall under each part of the curve.

14.   If two normal distributions have different means and variances then one way to compare scores across these two distributions is to convert the scores to _____ scores or _____ scores.

15.   If we calculate the difference between an individual score and the mean of the distribution from which the score was taken, and then divide this difference by the standard deviation of the distribution, the resulting score represents a _____ score.

MULTIPLE CHOICE QUESTIONS

_____ 1. Descriptive statistics
        a. summarize experimental observations.
        b. tell which data are important.
        c. indicate which differences are reliable.
        d. all of the above

_____ 2. The mean is:
        a. the same as the arithmetic average.
        b. the middle score.
        c. the most common score.
        d. the standard score.
        e. the extreme score.

_____ 3. The median is:

    a. the sum of scores divided by the number of scores.

    b. the most frequent score.

    c. the midpoint of the distribution of scores.

    d. the range of scores.

_____ 4. The primary reason the median is used is because

    a. it is the most useful measure of central tendency.

    b. it has the property of being insensitive to extreme scores.

    c. it has the property of accurately reflecting the range of scores.

    d. almost all inferential statistics are based on it.

_____ 5. The _____ is the most frequent score in a distribution.

    a. mode

    b. median

    c. mean

    d. range

_____ 6. What is the mode of this distribution?

    1 3 4 4 6 9 11 12 15

    a. 6

    b. 7.2

    c. 4

    d. 14

_____ 7. The simplest measure of dispersion in a group of scores is the:

    a. mode.

    b. range.

    c. standard deviation.

    d. variance.

    e. z-score.

_____ 8. A defining characteristic of the mean is that

    a. as n increases, the mean increases.

    b. the sum of the deviations of scores about the mean is always zero.

    c. the mean deviation equals the mean divided by $\underline{n}$.

    d. the mean is always less than the range.

_____ 9. The variance of a distribution is defined as the _____ divided by the number of scores.

    a. sum of the absolute deviations from the mean

    b. differences between the highest and lowest scores

    c. sum of the squared deviations from the mean

    d. sum of the absolute deviations from the median

_____10. The square root of the variance is the

    a. standard deviation.

    b. average deviation.

    c. mean deviation.

    d. sample deviation.

_____11. In describing an array of data, psychologists typically present two descriptive statistics, which are

    a. the median and variance.

    b. the median and standard deviation.

    c. the mean and the variance.

    d. the mean and the standard deviation.

_____12. Which of the following is a characteristic of the standard normal distribution?

    a. The mean, median, and mode are the same.

    b. The mean and median only are the same.

    c. The median and mode only are the same.

    d. The mean and mode only are the same.

    e. none of the above

_____13. Approximately what percentage of scores in a normal distribution fall between plus and minus one standard deviation from the mean?

    a. 17%

    b. 34%

    c. 68%

    d. 96%

    e. 99.7%

_____14. Approximately what percentage of scores in a normal distribution have z values between -2.0 and +2.0?

    a. 17%

    b. 34%

    c. 68%

    d. 96%

    e. 99.7%

TRUE-FALSE QUESTIONS

_____ 1. Another name for a histogram is a frequency polygon.

_____ 2. The most common measure of central tendency in psychological research is the mean.

_____ 3. Extremely small or large scores have an effect on the mean, but not on the mode or median.

_____ 4. The mean of a set of scores has the property that the deviations from the mean add up to zero.

_____ 5. The standard deviation is simply the square root of the variance.

_____ 6. A property of the standard normal distribution is that the mean and the median are the same, but the mode is different.

_____ 7. A z score is the difference between an individual score and the mean expressed in units of standard deviation.

Appendix B

Inferential Statistics

SUMMARY

Inferential statistics allow us to make inferences regarding the reliability of the observed differences among groups or conditions. From a research study we obtain a sample of scores and we want to infer from this sample what the results would be for the entire population(s) involved. While there is a wide variety of statistical tests available for making such inferences, the same logic is applied in all. An alternative hypothesis is tested against the null hypothesis which states that there are no differences between the groups or conditions. Specific computations are then performed that result in a numerical value that is then compared to a distribution of values in a table that informs us as to what level of confidence we can have in rejecting the null hypothesis.

A number of statistical tests are described that are appropriate for making various comparisons between groups. These include comparing experimental and control groups involving two independent groups (Mann-Whitney U test) or involving a within-subjects design or a matched-groups design (sign test and Wilcoxin signed-ranks test). For more complicated designs in which there are more than two groups to be compared the analysis of variance procedure is appropriate.

KEY TERMS

alpha level	parametric tests
analysis of variance	population
between-groups variance	power of a statistical test
degrees of freedom	qualitative variation
directional test	quantitative variation
distribution of sample means	repeated-measures design
experimental hypothesis	replacement
F-test	sample
inferential statistics	simple (one factor) analysis of variance
interaction effect	standard error of the mean
main effect	statistics
Mann-Whitney U-test	sum of squares
mean squares	two-tailed test
nondirectional test	Type-I error
nonparametric tests	Type-II error
null hypothesis	Wilcoxin signed ranks test
one-tailed test	within-group variance
parameters	

PROGRAMMED REVIEW

1. A complete set of measurements (or individual or objects) having some common observable characteristic is called a _____.

2. A subset of a population is called a _____.

3. If we conducted an experiment and then replicated that same experiment many times, the distribution of the resultant sample means would tend to be a _____ distribution.

4. The standard deviation of a distribution of sample means is called the _____ of the _____.

5. In general we want the standard error of the mean to be as _____ as possible. One way to do this is to _____ the size of the sample.

6. In testing hypotheses we pit the _____ hypothesis against the _____ hypothesis.

7. The null hypothesis predicts that _____

_____

8. If we know the standard deviation of the population then we can find the standard error of the mean by dividing the population standard deviation by _____

_____

9. If you are told that an observed difference was significant at the .05 level of confidence then this means that _____

_____

10. Rejecting the null hypothesis when it is actually true is called a Type _____ error, and the probability that this error is being made is indexed by the _____ level.

11. If we fail to reject the null hypothesis when it is in fact false, then we have committed a Type _____ error.

12. A conservative statistical test minimizes Type _____ errors.

13. The _____ of a test is the probability of rejecting the null hypothesis when it is actually false.

14. By increasing the _____ _____ we may increase the power of our test.

15. If the alternative hypothesis specifies the direction of the expected difference, then a _____-tailed test is used, but if the alternative hypothesis is nondirectional then a _____-tailed test is used.

16. Two-tailed tests are more _____ and _____ powerful than one-tailed tests.

17. A _____ statistical test is one that makes assumptions about the underlying population parameters of the samples on which the tests are performed.

18. In general _____ tests are less powerful than _____ tests employed in the same situation.

19. The Mann-Whitney U test is used to analyze data from a _____-subject design. The Wilcoxin signed-ranks test is used to analyze data from a _____-_____ design.

20. If a researcher used four levels of an independent variable and tested four separate groups of subjects, an appropriate statistical test for analyzing the data from this experiment would be a simple _____ _____ _____.

21. The F-test used in the analysis of variance is a ratio of the _____-groups variance estimate to the _____-groups variance estimate.

22. The null hypothesis predicts that the F-ratio should be _____.

23. In an experiment in which more than one factor is varied simultaneously the appropriate procedure for analyzing the results would be to use a _____ analysis of variance.

MULTIPLE CHOICE QUESTIONS

_____ 1. Inferential statistics are concerned with

    a. the importance of data.

    b. the meaning of data.

    c. the reliability of data.

    d. all of the above

_____ 2. Characteristics of a population of scores are called _____, while characteristics of a sample of scores drawn from a larger population are _____.

    a. statistics; parameters

    b. parameters; statistics

    c. generalizations; data

    d. inferences; facts

_____ 3. The distribution of sample means tends to be

    a. normal.

    b. exponential.

    c. Poisson.

    d. random.

_____ 4. The standard error of the mean is the

    a. square root of the mean.

    b. mean of a distribution of sample means

    c. variance of a distribution of sample means

    d. standard deviation of a distribution of sample means

_____ 5. The standard error of the mean represents the error we have in assuming that

    a. the mean represents the sample mean.

    b. the sample mean represents the population mean.

    c. the standard deviation of the sample mean is accurate.

    d. the standard deviation of the population mean is accurate.

_____ 6. As the sample size (n) increases,

    a. the sample mean increases.

    b. the standard error of the mean increases.

    c. the standard error of the mean decreases.

    d. the standard deviation of the mean increases.

_____ 7. The null hypothesis suggests that

    a. the two samples come from the same distribution.

    b. the two samples come from different distributions.

    c. the two samples come from different but overlapping. distributions.

    d. the two samples come from different but similar distributions.

_____ 8. Adopting a .05 level of confidence means that you would

    a. accept the null hypothesis if the results could occur 5 times in 100 by chance.

    b. reject the null hypothesis if the results could occur 5 times in 100 by chance.

    c. reject the experimental hypothesis if the results could occur 5 times in 100 by chance.

    d. none of the above

_____ 9. An experimental psychologist reports that his statistical test indicates that the difference between his experimental and control group in his latest experiment is highly significant. By this he means that

    a. the difference was highly unlikely to have occurred by chance.

    b. the difference was probably due to chance factors.

    c. the results are very important.

    d. both a and c

_____10. Rejecting the null hypothesis when it is actually true
is

a. a Type I error.

b. a Type II error.

c. a Type III error.

d. a standard error.

e. not an error; it's the right thing to do.

_____11. A Type I error occurs when you:

a. reject a false null hypothesis.

b. reject a true null hypothesis.

c. reject a true experimental hypothesis.

d. accept a false null hypothesis.

_____12. In hypothesis testing, both magnitude of the difference
and the direction of the difference between two groups
are considered in

a. two-tailed tests.

b. one-tailed tests.

c. parametric tests.

d. nonparametric tests.

_____13. Parametric tests

a. do not make assumptions about the underlying
population parameters.

b. make assumptions about the underlying population
parameters.

c. are typically more powerful than nonparametric
tests.

d. both b and c

_____14. Mann-Whitney U test can only be used for

a. within-subjects designs.

b. between-subjects designs.

c. repeated measures designs.

d. none of the above

TRUE-FALSE QUESTIONS

_____ 1. A population is a complete set of measurements (or individuals or objects) having some common observable characteristics.

_____ 2. The distribution of sample means is not a normal distribution.

_____ 3. As the sample size (n) increases, the standard error of the mean decreases, the power of the statistical test increases, and the probability of a Type II error decreases.

_____ 4. The null hypothesis maintains that the two samples of scores (experimental and control) come from two different underlying distributions.

_____ 5. Adopting a .05 level of confidence means that you would accept the null hypothesis if the obtained difference could occur 5 times in 100 by chance.

_____ 6. A Type I error is rejecting the null hypothesis when it is actually true.

_____ 7. A liberal statistical test minimizes the probability of making a Type II error.

_____ 8. One way to increase the power of a statistical test is to increase the sample size.

_____ 9. A two-tailed statistical test considers both the magnitude of the difference and the direction of the differences between two groups.

_____ 10. Nonparametric tests are those that make assumptions about the underlying population parameters while parametric tests do not make such assumptions.

_____ 11. A simple analysis of variance (ANOVA) uses only one dependent variable whereas a complex or multifactor ANOVA uses more than one dependent variable.

_____ 12. In an analysis of variance, the F ratio under the null hypothesis should equal 0.00.

Chapter 1 - Programmed Review

 1. behavior (p. 1)

 2. explanations; practical problems (p. 6)

 3. critic (p. 8)

 4. independent variable (p. 8)

 5. dependent variable (p. 8)

 6. control variables (p .8)

 7. confounding (p. 8)

 8. observation (p. 10)

 9. experts (p. 10)

10. *Psychological Abstracts* (p. 11)

11. testable hypothesis (p. 13)

12. observable; measurable (p. 13)

13. literature search (p. 14)

14. pilot (p. 15)

Multiple Choice Questions

1.	b (p. 1)	8.	b (p. 8)	14.	e (p. 12)
2.	c (p. 1)	9.	c (p. 8)	15.	d (p. 11)
3.	a (p. 5)	10.	d (p. 8)	16.	d (p. 13)
4.	c (p. 5)	11.	c (p. 9)	17.	d (p. 13)
5.	d (p. 6)	12.	d (p. 10-11)	18.	c (p. 14-15)
6.	a (p. 8)	13.	c (p. 12)	19.	d (p. 15-16)
7.	a (p. 8)				

True-False Questions

1.	F (p. 8)	3.	F (p. 9)	5.	F (p. 11)
2.	T (p. 6)	4.	T (p. 9)	6.	T (p. 13)

Chapter 2 - Programmed Review

1. social loafing (p. 26)
2. diffusion; responsibility (p. 26)
3. authority (p. 27)
4. tenacity (p. 28)
5. experience (p. 28)
6. empirical; self (p. 28)
7. data; theory (p. 29)
8. data; theory; deductive (p. 29)
9. inductive (p. 29)
10. deductive (p. 30)
11. testable (p. 30)
12. strong inference (p. 33)
13. organize (p. 33)
14. predictions (p. 33)
15. description; explanation (p. 34)
16. intervening variable (p. 35)
17. economy (p. 36)
18. precise (p. 38)
19. parsimony (p. 37)
20. precision (p. 38)

21. tested (p. 38)
22. techniques (p. 39)

MULTIPLE CHOICE QUESTIONS

1.	c (p. 26)	10.	b (p. 29)	18.	c (p. 36)
2.	d (p. 27)	11.	a (p. 30)	19.	c (p. 38)
3.	b (p. 27)	12.	d (p. 31-32)	20.	c (p. 38)
4.	a (p. 27)	13.	a (p. 30)	21.	d (p. 37-38)
5.	a (p. 28)	14.	c (p. 30)	22.	b (p. 38)
6.	b (p. 28)	15.	d (p. 33)	23.	c (p. 38)
7.	d (p. 28)	16.	d (p. 33)	24.	b (p. 39)
8.	d (p. 28)	17.	c (p. 35)	25.	c (p. 41)
9.	a (p. 29)				

TRUE-FALSE QUESTIONS

1.	T (p. 27)	9.	F (p. 30)	16.	F (p. 38)
2.	F (p. 27)	10.	T (p. 30)	17.	F (p. 38)
3.	T (p. 28)	11.	F (p. 34)	18.	T (p. 38)
4.	T (p. 28)	12.	F (p. 35)	19.	F (p. 40)
5.	T (p. 29)	13.	F (p. 36)	20.	F (p. 40)
6.	F (p. 30)	14.	T (p. 37)	21.	F (p. 41)
7.	T (p. 30)	15.	T (p. 38)	22.	F (p. 41)
8.	T (p. 30)				

Chapter 3 - Programmed Review

1. validity (p. 49)
2. construct (p. 49)
3. confounding; random error (p. 49)
4. operational definition; construct (p. 50)
5. protocol (p. 50)
6. external (p. 51)
7. replicate (p. 51)
8. internal validity (p. 51)
9. confounding (p. 52)
10. descriptive (p. 54)

11. naturalistic observations; case study; survey (p. 54)

12. database (p. 54)

13. related (p. 59)

14. replicated (p. 59)

15. anthropomorphizing (p. 59)

16. correlation coefficient (p. 60)

17. predict (p. 60)

18. -1.0; +1.0 (p. 61)

19. stronger (p. 61)

20. direction (p. 61)

21. scatter diagram (p. 62)

22. causal (p. 63)

23. third variable (p. 63)

24. low (p. 65)

25. crossed-lagged-panel (p. 66)

26. experimental (p. 69)

MULTIPLE CHOICE QUESTIONS

1.	b (p. 49)	8.	c (p. 51)	14.	a (p. 59)
2.	a (p. 49)	9.	d (p. 49,51)	15.	a (p. 59)
3.	a (p. 49)	10.	c (p. 54)	16.	a (p. 60)
4.	c (p. 50)	11.	a (p. 55)	17.	b (p. 61)
5.	a (p. 50)	12.	a (p. 57)	18.	c (p. 66)
6.	b (p. 51)	13.	d (p. 58)	19.	c (p. 88)
7.	b (p. 51)				

TRUE-FALSE QUESTIONS

1.	T (p. 49)	8.	F (p. 51)	14.	F (p. 59)
2.	F (p. 49)	9.	F (p. 54)	15.	F (p. 61)
3.	F (p. 49)	10.	T (p. 54)	16.	F (p. 61)
4.	T (p. 50)	11.	T (p. 55)	17.	F (p. 61)
5.	F (p. 51)	12.	F (p. 55)	18.	F (p. 61)
6.	F (p. 51)	13.	T (p. 59)	19.	F (p. 61)
7.	T (p. 51)				

Chapter 4 - Programmed Review

1. measurement (p. 75)
2. nominal (p. 77)
3. differences; ordinal (p. 77)
4. interval; equal intervals (p. 77)
5. ratio; true zero (p. 78)
6. ordinal; interval (p. 78)
7. reliability (p. 79)
8. test-retest (p. 80)
9. split-half (p. 80)
10. inferential; statistically reliable (p. 81)
11. power; increasing (p. 82)
12. random (p. 82)
13. increase (p. 82)
14. experimental (p. 83)
15. physical (p. 85)
16. psychophysical method; thresholds (p. 85)
17. absolute threshold (p. 87)
18. difference; relative; changing (p. 87)
19. interval; uncertainty (p. 88)
20. point; subjective equality (p. 88)
21. constant (p. 88)
22. threshold (p. 89)
23. intensity; just-noticeable differences (p. 90)
24. log (p. 91)
25. indirectly; directly; magnitude estimation (p. 91)
26. power (p. 91)
27. ordinate; abscissa (p. 93)
28. independent (p. 93)
29. nominal (p. 94)

MULTIPLE CHOICE QUESTIONS

1.	d	(p. 76)	10.	c	(p. 83)	18.	d	(p. 88)
2.	d	(p. 76)	11.	a	(p. 83)	19.	c	(p. 88)
3.	d	(p. 76)	12.	a	(p. 83)	20.	b	(p. 88)
4.	b	(p. 77)	13.	c	(p. 85)	21.	b	(p. 90)
5.	c	(p. 77)	14.	a	(p. 86)	22.	c	(p. 91)
6.	b	(p. 79)	15.	d	(p. 86)	23.	b	(p. 91)
7.	c	(p. 81)	16.	c	(p. 86)	24.	b	(p. 91)
8.	a	(p. 82)	17.	b	(p. 87)	25.	b	(p. 93)
9.	b	(p. 82)						

TRUE-FALSE QUESTIONS

1.	T	(p. 78)	8.	T	(p. 83)	15.	T	(p. 89)
2.	F	(p. 77)	9.	T	(p. 83)	16.	T	(p. 89)
3.	T	(p. 78)	10.	T	(p. 83)	17.	T	(p. 91)
4.	F	(p. 77)	11.	T	(p. 85)	18.	T	(p. 93)
5.	T	(p. 79)	12.	F	(p. 87)	19.	F	(p. 94)
6.	F	(p. 80)	13.	T	(p. 86)	20.	F	(p. 96)
7.	F	(p. 81)	14.	F	(p. 88)			

Chapter 5 - Programmed Review

1. picture; initials (p. 103,104)
2. cause (p. 105)
3. joint method of agreement and difference (p. 105)
4. comparison; independent; experimental setting (p. 106,107)
5. independent, dependent, control (p. 109-11)
6. experimental (p. 108)
7. independent (p. 108)
8. control (p. 108)
9. change (p. 109)
10. null result (p. 109)
11. null results (p. 109)
12. independent (p. 110)
13. reliable (p. 110)

14. null (p. 110)

15. floor; ceiling (p. 111)

16. small (p. 111)

17. constant (p. 111)

18. increases (p. 111)

19. more (p. 114)

20. valid (p. 114)

21. interaction (p. 114)

22. presence of birthmark; presence of intern (p. 114,115)

23. interaction (p. 115,116)

24. multivariate (p. 118)

25. one; two (p. 117)

MULTIPLE CHOICE QUESTIONS

1.   b (p. 104)   8. a (p. 109)   14. e (p. 107)

2.   c (p. 105)   9. e (p. 109,110) 15. b (p. 111)

3.   c (p. 106)   10. a (p. 110)   16. a (p. 114)

4.   a (p. 107)   11. d (p. 111)   17. d (p. 109-11)

5.   a (p. 108)   12. a (p. 111)   18. d (p. 114)

6.   b (p. 108)   13. d (p. 114)   19. a (p. 116)

7.   d (p. 109)

TRUE-FALSE QUESTIONS

1.   T (p. 108)   5.   F (p. 108)   9.   F (p. 114)

2.   F (p. 105)   6.   F (p. 109)   10. T (p. 114)

3.   F (p. 105)   7.   T (p. 110)   11. T (p. 116)

4.   T (p. 108)   8.   T (p. 111)

Chapter 6 - Programmed Review

  1. caused (p. 122)

  2. internally (p. 122)

  3. whether or not monkeys could postpone shock (p. 122)

  4. high (p. 123)

  5. within (p. 123)

6.   subjects (p. 124)

7.   between (p. 124)

8.   treatment groups (p. 125)

9.   subject (p. 126)

10.   confounding (p. 126)

11.   attrition (p. 126)

12.   randomization (p. 126)

13.   arranging (p. 127)

14.   randomization (p. 127)

15.   within (p. 127)

16.   carryover (p. 127)

17.   subjects (p. 128)

18.   counterbalancing (p. 128)

19.   Latin Square (p. 130)

20.   odd (p. 130)

21.   mixed (p. 133)

22.   control (p. 131)

23.   baseline (p. 133)

24.   between-subjects (p. 133)

25.   within-subjects (p. 134)

Multiple Choice Questions

1.	a	(p. 122)	7.	b	(p. 125)	12.	c	(p. 128)
2.	b	(p. 123)	8.	e	(p. 126)	13.	d	(p. 130)
3.	c	(p. 123)	9.	a	(p. 126)	14.	b	(p. 133)
4.	e	(p. 124)	10.	b	(p. 126)	15.	b	(p. 132)
5.	b	(p. 125)	11.	c	(p. 128)	16.	c	(p. 132)
6.	b	(p. 127)						

True-False Questions

1.	T	(p. 122)	6.	F	(p. 128)	11.	F	(p. 128)
2.	T	(p. 127)	7.	T	(p. 126)	12.	F	(p. 130)
3.	F	(p. 124)	8.	T	(p. 126)	13.	T	(p. 131)
4.	F	(p. 125)	9.	F	(p. 126)	14.	T	(p. 131)
5.	F	(p. 133)	10.	T	(p. 127)	15.	T	(P. 134)

Chapter 7 - Programmed Review

1. ecological (p. 141)
2. internal (p. 141)
3. sleeper (p. 142)
4. discounting cue (p. 142)
5. independent; levels (p. 142)
6. independent variable (p. 142)
7. main (p. 143)
8. interaction (p. 144)
9. selected; assigned (p. 148)
10. subjects (p. 148)
11. randomly; Latin square (p. 149)
12. confounding (p. 149)
13. random; groups (p. 149)
14. subjects (p. 149)
15. within (p. 150)
16. within; between (p. 150)
17. subject (p. 150)
18. 2; 1 (p. 151)
19. carryover (p. 153)
20. counterbalancing; blocked (p. 153)
21. blocked (p. 154)
22. mixed (p. 155)
23. between (p. 155)
24. repeated measures (p. 155)
25. trials (p. 156)
26. extinction (p. 157)

Multiple Choice Questions

1.	c	(p. 141)	9.	d	(p. 144)	16.	e	(p. 150)
2.	e	(p. 142)	10.	a	(p. 146)	17.	e	(p. 150)
3.	b	(p. 142)	11.	d	(p. 144-6)	18.	c	(p. 151-3)
4.	c	(p. 142)	12.	b	(p. 141)	19.	d	(p. 155)
5.	c	(p. 142)	13.	c	(p. 142-4)	20.	e	(p. 151-2)
6.	a	(p. 144)	14.	e	(p. 147)	21.	a	(p. 154)
7.	b	(p. 144)	15.	a	(p. 148)	22.	c	(p. 157)
8.	b	(p. 142)						

TRUE-FALSE QUESTIONS

1.	T	(p. 141)	5.	F	(p. 146)	9.	T	(p. 153)
2.	F	(p. 141)	6.	F	(p. 144)	10.	T	(p. 154)
3.	F	(p. 150)	7.	F	(p. 149)	11.	T	(p. 154)
4.	F	(p. 143)	8.	F	(p. 150)			

Chapter 8 - Programmed Review

1. subjects (p. 163)
2. threshold (p. 164)
3. sensory impressions; decision (p. 164)
4. costs; benefits (p. 164)
5. noise (p. 165)
6. distribution; sensory (p. 165)
7. noise; signal; noise (p. 165)
8. criterion; criterion; decision (p. 165)
9. hit; false alarm (p. 165)
10. receiver; operating (p. 166)
11. sensitivity; distance between (p. 167)
12. beta; slope (p. 167)
13. criterion; $\underline{d}'$ (p. 167)
14. baseline; independent (p. 169)
15. time (p. 169)
16. reversal (p. 169)
17. independent; dependent variable (p. 170)

18. independent; B (p. 170)
19. extinguish; rewarding (p. 170)
20. increased; baseline; decreased; extinction (p. 170)
21. long; term (p. 171)
22. independent; dependent (p. 171)
23. case study (p. 173)
24. would be (p. 173)
25. would not be (p. 173)

Multiple Choice Questions

1.	d	(p. 163)	7.	c	(p. 165)	13.	a	(p. 169)
2.	c	(p. 163)	8.	c	(p. 167)	14.	e	(p. 170)
3.	c	(p. 164)	9.	b	(p. 167)	15.	b	(p. 169)
4.	b	(p. 166)	10.	a	(p. 167)	16.	c	(p. 172)
5.	b	(p. 165)	11.	a	(p. 169)	17.	c	(p. 173)
6.	a	(p. 165)	12.	c	(p. 170)	18.	b	(p. 173)

TRUE-FALSE QUESTIONS

1.	T	(p. 163)	4.	F	(p. 164)	7.	T	(p. 169)
2.	F	(p. 163)	5.	T	(p. 167)	8.	T	(p. 169)
3.	T	(p. 164)	6.	T	(p. 166)	9.	F	(p. 173)

Chapter 9 - Programmed Review

1. unethical (p. 179)
2. ABA (p. 199)
3. (a) The treatment is not under the experimenter's control.
     (b) Most natural treatments have long carryover effects
          (p. 180)
4. history; subject (p. 180)
5. match (p. 180)
6. control condition (p. 181)
7. number (p. 182)
8. mortality; selection (p. 184)
9. effect (p. 184)

10. subject (p. 186)

11. correlations (p. 187)

12. confounded (p. 187)

13. matching (p. 188)

14. sample (p. 188)

15. additive; interact (p. 188)

16. regression (p. 189)

17. longitudinal (p. 191)

18. cross sectional (p. 191)

19. independent (p. 191)

20. cohort (p. 191)

21. testing; age (p. 191)

Multiple Choice Questions

1.	b	(p. 179)	7.	c	(p. 179)	13.	a	(p. 188)
2.	a	(p. 180)	8.	b	(p. 186)	14.	c	(p. 191)
3.	b	(p. 181)	9.	d	(p. 188)	15.	c	(p. 191)
4.	d	(p. 183)	10.	b	(p. 188)	16.	d	(p. 191)
5.	d	(p. 181)	11.	c	(p. 188)	17.	c	(p. 192)
6.	e	(p. 186)	12.	a	(p. 189)			

TRUE-FALSE QUESTIONS

1.	F	(p. 179)	8.	T	(p. 188)	15.	F	(p. 191)
2.	F	(p. 180)	9.	F	(p. 188)	16.	T	(p. 191)
3.	T	(p. 180)	10.	F	(p. 189)	17.	F	(p. 191)
4.	T	(p. 181)	11.	F	(p. 188)	18.	T	(p. 191)
5.	F	(p. 183)	12.	T	(p. 188)	19.	T	(p. 192)
6.	T	(p. 186)	13.	T	(p. 188)	20.	T	(p. 192)
7.	F	(p. 188)	14.	T	(p. 189)			

Chapter 10 - Programmed Review

1. reactive (p. 200)

2. observation; measurement (p. 200)

3. indirect (p. 201)

4. retrospective (p. 201)
5. motivated forgetting (p. 201)
6. styles; response (p. 202)
7. response styles (p. 202)
8. volunteer problem (p. 202)
9. Hawthorne effect (p. 204)
10. reactivity (p. 205)
11. good subject (p. 207)
12. field research (p. 208)
13. control (p. 208)
14. blind experiment (p. 208)
15. replication (p. 210)
16. blind (p. 212)
17. double-blind (p. 212)
18. placebo (p. 212)
19. anthropomorphizing (p. 213)
20. duplicate (p. 214)
21. make sense; copied (p. 215)
22. observed; operational definitions (p. 215)
23. valid (p. 216)
24. processes (p. 217)
25. variable representativeness (p. 218)
26. realism (p. 219)
27. field study (p. 219)
28. processes (p. 219)

Multiple Choice Questions

1.	b	(p. 201)	9.	c	(p. 203)	17.	c	(p. 208)
2.	d	(p. 201)	10.	a	(p. 203)	18.	a	(p. 209)
3.	c	(p. 202)	11.	c	(p. 203)	19.	e	(p. 212)
4.	a	(p. 202)	12.	a	(p. 204)	20.	e	(p. 212)
5.	c	(p. 200)	13.	e	(p. 205)	21.	a	(p. 214)
6.	b	(p. 200)	14.	e	(p. 207)	22.	d	(p. 219)
7.	e	(p. 202)	15.	b	(p. 207)	23.	a	(p. 221)
8.	b	(p. 202)	16.	a	(p. 208)			

True-False Questions

1.	T	(p. 200)	6.	F	(p. 203)	11. T	(p. 210)
2.	F	(p. 200)	7.	T	(p. 203)	12. F	(p. 211)
3.	T	(p. 201)	8.	T	(p. 204)	13. F	(p. 213)
4.	T	(p. 201)	9.	F	(p. 208)	14. T	(p. 218)
5.	F	(p. 202)	10.	F	(p. 209)		

Chapter 11 - Programmed Review

1. attenuation (p. 227)
2. ceiling; floor (p. 227)
3. visual; auditory (p. 229)
4. ceiling (p. 230)
5. pilot (p. 231)
6. difficulty (p. 231)
7. regression; mean (p. 232)
8. unreliability (p. 233)
9. populations (p. 234)
10. random assignment (p. 235)
11. large; repeatable (p. 236)
12. invalid (p. 236)
13. experimental (p. 236)
14. experimental (p. 237)
15. direct replication (p. 238)
16. systematic (p. 238)
17. converging operations (p. 240)
18. Stroop (p. 241)
19. increases (p. 241)
20. response competition; perceptual inhibition (p. 243)
21. how close the subject would let the experimenter approach (p. 243)
22. fewer (p. 244)

Multiple Choice Questions

1.	b	(p. 227)	8.	c	(p. 236)	14.	a	(p. 241)
2.	b	(p. 230)	9.	b	(p. 236)	15.	d	(p. 243)
3.	c	(p. 231)	10.	d	(p. 237)	16.	a	(p. 243)
4.	d	(p. 232)	11.	c	(p. 238)	17.	b	(p. 244)
5.	d	(p. 232)	12.	d	(p. 240)	18.	a	(p. 244)
6.	b	(p. 234)	13.	d	(p. 240)	19.	d	(p. 244)
7.	b	(p. 234,5)						

True-False Questions

1.	F	(p. 229)	7.	F	(p. 232)	13.	T	(p. 238)
2.	F	(p. 231)	8.	T	(p. 233)	14.	T	(p. 244)
3.	F	(p. 229)	9.	F	(p. 233)	15.	F	(p. 240)
4.	F	(p. 229)	10.	F	(p. 234)	16.	F	(p. 241)
5.	T	(p. 230)	11.	F	(p. 236)	17.	T	(p. 243)
6.	T	(p. 231)	12.	F	(p. 236)	18.	F	(p. 243)

Chapter 12 - Programmed Review

1. peer (p. 249)
2. before (p. 250)
3. harm (p. 251,2)
4. remove (p. 252)
5. dignity; welfare (p. 251)
6. withdrawing (p. 254)
7. physical; mental (p. 251)
8. internally (p. 252)
9. optional (p. 254)
10. debriefing (p. 254)
11. confidential (p. 255)
12. empirical (p. 256)
13. speciesism (p. 258)
14. costs; benefits (p. 259)
15. human; animal (p. 258)

Multiple Choice Questions

1. b (p. 252)   4. a (p. 252)   6. e (p. 258)
2. d (p. 252-7)   5. b (p. 254)   7. c (p. 258)
3. d (p. 255)

True-False Questions

1. T (p. 249)   4. F (p. 253)   7. F (p. 255,6)
2. T (p. 251)   5. T (p. 254)   8. F (p. 256)
3. F (p. 250)   6. F (p. 254)

Chapter 13 - Programmed Review

 1. a) title; author(s) (p. 269)
     b) abstract
     c) introduction
     d) method
     e) results
     f) discussion
     g) references
 2. Publication Manual (p. 269)
 3. dependent; independent (p. 270)
 4. abstract (p. 270)
 5. end (p. 270)
 6. hypothesis; predictions (p. 270)
 7. method (p. 271)
 8. subjects; apparatus; procedure (p. 271)
 9. results (p. 271)
10. scales (p. 273)
11. discussion (p. 273)
12. hypothesis; assumptions (p. 275)
13. experiment; hypothesis (p. 275)
14. hypothesis (p. 275)
15. results (p. 276)
16. title; name(s); affiliation; running head (p. 285)
17. abstract (p. 285)

18. cover-page; introduction (p. 285)
19. references (p. 285)
20. transitions (p. 308)
21. past; present (p. 310)

Multiple Choice Questions

1. e (p. 269)   5. e (p. 273)   8. d (p. 276)
2. d (p. 270)   6. b (p. 275)   9. e (p. 276-7)
3. d (p. 271)   7. c (p. 276)   10. b (p. 285)
4. a (p. 271)

True-False Questions

1. F (p. 270)   4. F (p. 273)   6. T (p. 310)
2. F (p. 271)   5. F (p. 276)   7. T (p. 311)
3. T (p. 273)

Appendix A - Programmed Review

1. central tendency; dispersion (p. 317)
2. histogram (p. 317)
3. frequency polygon (p. 317)
4. arithmetic mean (p. 318)
5. median; mode (p. 318,319)
6. median (p. 319)
7. range (p. 319)
8. absolute (p. 320)
9. variance (p. 321)
10. standard deviation (p. 320)
11.
$$\frac{\sum (X-\overline{X})^2}{n}$$ (p. 321)

12. mean; standard deviation (p. 320)
13. proportion (p. 323)
14. standard; _z_ (p. 324)
15. standard (p. 324)

Multiple Choice Questions

1.	a (p. 317)	6.	c (p. 319)	11.	d (p. 321)
2.	a (p. 318)	7.	c (p. 319)	12.	a (p. 322)
3.	c (p. 318)	8.	c (p. 320)	13.	c (p. 323)
4.	b (p. 319)	9.	b (p. 321)	14.	d (p. 323)
5.	a (p. 319)	10.	a (p. 321)		

True-False Questions

1.	F (p. 317)	4.	T (p. 320)	6.	F (p. 322)
2.	T (p. 318)	5.	T (p. 321)	7.	T (p. 324)
3.	T (p. 319)				

Appendix B - Programmed Review

1. population (p. 329)
2. sample (p. 330)
3. normal (p. 331)
4. standard error; mean (p. 332)
5. small; increase (p. 332)
6. null; experimental (p. 334)
7. there is no difference between the experimental and control conditions (p. 334)
8. square root of the sample size (p. 332)
9. the observed difference could happen by chance only 5 times in 100. (p. 336)
10. I; alpha (p. 337)
11. II (p. 337)
12. I (p. 337)
13. power (p. 337)
14. sample size (p. 337,8)
15. one; two (p. 338)
16. conservative; less (p. 339)
17. parametric (p. 341)
18. nonparametric; parametric (p. 340)
19. between; repeated measures (p. 341,2)

20. analysis of variance (p. 348)
21. between; within (p. 348)
22. 1.00 (p. 341)
23. multifactor (p. 347)

Multiple Choice Questions

1.	c	(p. 329)	6.	c	(p. 333)	11.	b	(p. 337)
2.	b	(p. 330)	7.	a	(p. 334)	12.	b	(p. 338)
3.	a	(p. 331)	8.	b	(p. 337)	13.	b	(p. 341)
4.	d	(p. 332)	9.	a	(p. 337)	14.	b	(p. 341)
5.	b	(p. 332)	10.	a	(p. 337)			

True-False Questions

1.	T	(p. 329)	5.	F	(p. 337)	9.	T	(p. 338)
2.	F	(p. 331)	6.	T	(p. 337)	10.	F	(p. 341)
3.	T	(p. 334-8)	7.	T	(p. 337)	11.	F	(p. 347)
4.	F	(p. 334)	8.	T	(p. 337-8)	12.	F	(p. 348)